The End of
the Modern World

ROMANO GUARDINI

Introduction by
Frederick D. Wilhelmsen

Foreword by
Richard John Neuhaus

ISI BOOKS
INTERCOLLEGIATE STUDIES INSTITUTE
WILMINGTON, DELAWARE
1998

© Copyright 1956, Translated by Joseph Theman and Herbert Burke, Sheed & Ward, Inc.

© Copyright 1961, Translated by Elinor C. Briefs, Henry Regnery Company

Nihil Obstat: Rt. Rev.

Msgr. J. Gerald Kealy, *Censor Deputatus.*

Imprimatur: Albert Cardinal Meyer, S.T.D., S.S.L.,

Archiepiscopus Chicagienis, October 27, 1960.

Foreword © Copyright 1998, ISI Books

Revised Edition, 1998, ISI Books

Second Paperback Printing, 2013, ISI Books

Library of Congress Catalog Card Numbers 56-9526, 61-7963

Cataloging-in-Publication Data

Guardini, Romano, 1885-1968.

The end of the modern world / Romano Guardini;

introduction by Frederick D. Wilhelmsen;

foreword by Richard John Neuhaus.– [Rev. ed.] –

Wilmington, DE: ISI Books, 2001, c 1998.

p. cm.

Previously published separately as: The end of the modern world; and, Power and responsibility.

ISBN 1-882926-58-7 (pbk.)

1. Church and the world–History of doctrine. 2. Man (Christian theology) I. Guardini, Romano, 1885-1968. Power and responsibility. II. Title.

| BR115.W6 G83 2001 | 00-110949 |
| 261/.2–dc21 | CIP |

Published in the United States by:

ISI Books,

3901 Centerville Road,

Wilmington, DE 19807

www.isibooks.org

Manufactured in the United States of America

The End of
the Modern World

To My Brothers

Mario and Aleardo

CONTENTS

Foreword by Richard John Neuhaus..IX

Introduction by Frederick D. Wilhelmsen..XIII

Author's Introduction...XXIV

I. THE END OF THE MODERN WORLD:

A Search for Orientation

1. THE SENSE OF BEING AND THE WORLD PICTURE

   OF THE MIDDLE AGES...1

2. THE BIRTH OF THE MODERN WORLD............................28

3. THE DISSOLUTION OF THE MODERN WORLD

   AND THE WORLD WHICH IS TO COME....................................50

II. POWER AND RESPONSIBILITY:

A Course of Action for the New Age

4. THE ESSENCE OF POWER..117

5. THE THEOLOGICAL CONCEPT OF POWER........................131

6. THE UNFOLDING OF POWER..149

7. THE NEW CONCEPT OF THE WORLD AND OF MAN.........170

8. POSSIBILITIES OF ACTION..208

There are writers whom you read because you're told you must read them. Having done so, they then become part of your history, along with foreign countries you have visited or great music you have heard. It's all part of the never-ending process called learning, and a very good thing it is. But then there are writers who catch you up short.

They are personally disruptive; intellectually and spiritually disruptive. They cannot be fitted into anything so smoothly incremental as a "process." Their claims demand a decision, and contingent upon that decision is a change of disposition toward a host of questions. The thought cannot be resisted: "If he's right about this, then I have to rethink an awful lot that follows from this."

Romano Guardini is such a writer. As he writes toward the end of the present volume, his purpose is "to declare a truth when its 'hour' has come." Guardini is frequently depicted as a conservative opponent of modernity who invokes a curse on all its ways and all its pomps. That depiction is not devoid of truth, for certainly there is a fine polemical edge—and sometimes a bludgeon—in much that he would declare. Polemics are sometimes necessary to catch attention and clear the air of cant, but Guardini is up to much more than polemics. He is proposing a different way of discovering one's "location" in the world; a different way of standing before history and, finally, before God. He does not posit—as some conservatives, especially Catholic conservatives, do—a "premodern" alternative to modernity. His keen historical consciousness allows no alternative to both the benefits and ravages of the time of which we are inescapably part. The only alternative to past and present is a future that is ultimately open to a better way of being human, if we have the nerve and imagination for it.

At the beginning of the third millennium, the cultural air is filled with expectations both hopeful and catastrophic. With respect to the human prospect, Guardini may be viewed as a pessimist, but I think that is to miss the point. Optimism and pessimism are the wrong categories altogether. Optimism is finally just a matter of optics, of seeing what we want to see and not seeing what we don't want to see; and pessimism is its twin. Guardini's view of the future is admittedly bleak at times, and little that has happened in the years since he wrote these pages would likely change that. But his is a disposition toward a hope that is unblinking in the face of all the reasons for despair. His hero—the kind of man he intended to be and invites his reader to be—is not unlike Kierkegaard's "knight of faith." The question is not whether the glass is half full or half empty, but what do you do when you know it's empty.

Guardini is brutal in his demolition of sentimental faith in gods such as Man, Nature, and History. Such religions are consigned, as Marx might say, to the dustbin of history. In Guardini's view, there is a devastating discontinuity between how people once "located" themselves in the world and our present circumstance. In the fine phrase of contemporary theologian Robert Jenson, "The world has lost its story."

Not only the Jewish-Christian story, but all the other stories that fed off that story, such as the story of progress. Guardini urges us not to be like Nietzsche's pitiful "last man" who never got the news that the jig is up. The old stories are exhausted, contends Guardini, they cannot be rehabilitated. There is nothing left for us now but to act upon, at long last, the invitation of Christ to rely on nothing but love. Not a sentimental love, but the harsh and dreadful love of the way of the cross.

I don't know whether or not Guardini is right. There is an alternative reading of our historical moment, in which the sentimental and bloody delusions of inevitable progress (*e.g.*, Marxism) have been decisively discredited, opening the world-historical stage to a fresh restatement of the Great Story that "locates" man in the working out of God's purposes against an horizon of eschatological promise. That alternative is set forth in many ways by, for instance, Pope John Paul II, and very notably in his encyclical on world evangelization, *Redemptoris Missio (The Mission of the Redeemer)*. Only God knows what the future holds, which is just as it should be. Guardini's great work can be seen as positing an alternative, maybe the alternative, to the world's rediscovering its story. And, of course, he may be right.

In any event, *The End of the Modern World* is bracing stuff. It offers welcome relief from fashionable post-modernisms that, in most instances, do no more than segue into the next phase of modernism. Romano Guardini insists that the music has stopped, even if some witless nostalgists keep humming the old tunes. What comes next, what has already arrived, is in radical discontinuity, something no earlier generation could have conceived, and something the wisest of us little understand. This is not a book to read and then check off one's list of "must reading." It is an engagement with a great mind and great spirit who will settle for nothing less than a decision. Upon that decision many other decisions inexorably follow.

Richard John Neuhaus
New York City
SS. Peter and Paul, 1998

INTRODUCTION

The End of the Modern World is the most somber book to come out of Germany since the Third Reich died in the bomb-pocked gardens of the Wilhelmstrasse. This book was begun in the afterglow from the holocaust of the idols of the nineteenth century. It was completed amidst the smoldering ashes of the twilight of the gods and it rings with the apocalyptic vision of the New Testament. For Romano Guardini writes of the end of our world. And he writes of the world which is to come.

Were I to find an historical parallel to Guardini's vision, I would find it in Saint Jerome's *Epistle* on the destruction of Gaul in which he declared:

> The mind shudders when dwelling on the ruin of our day. Roman blood has been flowing ceaselessly over the broad countries between Constantinople and the Julian Alps, where the Goths, the Huns and the Vandals spread ruin and death.... How many Roman nobles have been their prey! How many matrons and maidens have fallen victim to their lust! Bishops live in prison, priests and clerics fall by the sword, churches are plundered, Christ's altars are turned into feeding troughs, the remains of the martyrs are thrown out of their coffins. On every

side sorrow, on every side lamentation, everywhere the image of death.

But Guardini would reject my analogy. He would say
that the Germanic barbarians were absorbed into the
old Roman order, which they did not destroy but
transformed by their nervous genius. From this mingling of the mind of Latin antiquity with the vigor of
the Teutonic north was born a new civilization—that
Christendom which transcended by transfiguring the
old order that went before it.

But the world of our tomorrow, says Guardini, will
have nothing in common with the world of our yesterday. Until today the great historic eras through
which the West has passed have been in a living continuity with one another. Until the present our
civilization has reached for the future by mounting
the scaffolding of the past. Until now our common
forefathers maintained, from Virgil to Vico and from
Vico to Berdyaev, that history sustains—as part of
itself—a corporate memory that redeems death and
time and thus lifts them to the dignity of things eternal. And if this be true, if history really partakes of the
inherited civilization of our ancestors, then man today
has dropped history as a ship drops its pilot at Land's
End. From thenceforth, we sail in darkness.

The great historic eras through which the West has
passed are intelligible, says Guardini, because they
stand in a living continuity with one another. Medieval
man retained the limited Ptolemaic world he inherited from classical antiquity. Modern man retained

Christian values even when he secularized and thus debased them. But the man of the future will retain nothing from the past. Nowhere is this more sharply evident, according to Guardini, than in man's sense of his own place within the cosmos. The three ages of the West are marked off from one another exactly as man located himself within the universe of being. The word "located" is used deliberately and with the full force of its literal meaning. I would go so far as to say that if Aristotle is honored for writing the philosophy of *place,* Guardini will be honored for its theology. To say this is also to say that he has written its history. His thesis is that, for the first time in history, man has absolutely no place in the universe. This alone cuts the new age away from the modern world which has gone before it. Man no longer has a place, not merely in the theoretical sense that all hierarchic orders have disappeared in a collectivist society of mass men, but in the more profound sense that the universe of relativity physics has abolished the concept and the very reality of place itself. Man will continue to exist in the new world, but his existence will be condemned to rootlessness; he will be, but he will be nowhere. Nor will man find God within this new world. God is, but He will be nowhere.

Men of classical antiquity, on the contrary, had a well-defined place in the universe. They took their stance at the center of an earth that was the center of a universe composed of nine concentric spheres that turned cyclically in a movement that forever turned upon itself. Classical man, sailing across the

Adriatic on a star-filled night, looked up and saw a sky that was literally the vault of heaven. The world existed for the ancients exactly as they took it into their eyes. Man was at home in this world because it was as limited as is man himself. It was a world proportioned to a finite intellect and a finite sensibility. Beyond it there was nothing.

Medieval man retained this limited universe of his pagan forefathers, but he cracked its shell with the Christian Revelation and thus broke through to the Godhead. The Gothic in the springtime of its splendor lanced the Heart of God. And medieval man experienced this in the darkness of his Faith, which he buttressed with a natural symbolism built into the very substance of his being.

Before a reality—be it a reality of the Faith or of the cosmos—can exist for a man, it must take on a structure proportioned by the limits his senses place upon the realities conveyed to his intelligence. Guardini insists that nothing is *really* real for mankind until it can be located, until man can find it in some given place. Thus, we might add, man has always sought the divine in groves; he has always enshrined the sacred and fitted it to things human. Nothing exists for us unless we can point at it, if not in itself, at least in some symbol that we carve in space and that endures through time. For God to be a reality for man, He must exist somewhere. In the Middle Ages God lived in a definite place: just beyond the ninth sphere, in the Empyrean, that mysterious realm of light that surrounded the cosmos and closed the world. This place was Heaven itself.

Guardini's thesis may shock the mind educated exclusively in abstractions and theories. But if we meditate on the world in which we *really* live, the only world in which we have our being, then Guardini's assertion strikes home with the absolute rightness of one of those adamantine truths which are half-unseen because they are as light as the air and as elusive as the mist. To the senses, the sun truly rises in the east and sets in the west; the ship disappears beyond the line of the horizon; the moon turns slowly on its axis and thus reveals its many faces to the earth below; the stars beyond remain fixed to the arched roof of the sky. This is the world that moves us as does a lantern in the dark, a tower in the distance, a sentinel in the night: this is the world we know because it alone answers, as a friend, something too deep for words and too sacred for science. And before this world, all science is but shadow and symbol.

We exist in a medieval world. Nowhere is this more evident than in the life of prayer. In the prayer of praise and supplication man lifts his heart toward God by raising head and arms to the Lord on the Highest: *Gloria in excelsis Deo!* Thus the priest at the altar. In the prayer of contrition and repentance, man bows before the God of Justice and Mercy by lowering head to breast as he seeks Him within the depths of his heart: *Confiteor Deo!* Thus the priest at the foot of the altar. And St. Augustine says, "Where I am most inwardly myself, there You were far more than I." To find God in the depths of the soul, says Guardini, is to surmount the world simply because the God within is the same God who reigns beyond in His Heaven above. When man retreats within his soul searching for the God of his conscience, he swarms over the final barriers of the world and confronts there in the beyond a God seen in Faith and through a glass darkly. Guardini calls this an "immanence passing into transcendence," and although this mystery is wrought by grace, it finds its concrete representation in the vision of the cosmos which medieval man made his own. This vision fits the Christian at prayer.

But this world was rejected by degrees as modern man developed the Copernican and Newtonian universe. At the same time he was finding it psychologically more and more difficult to accept the Revelation that had transfigured the older cosmos. Modern man finally transferred the old sense of the Infinite from God to Nature. Instead of piercing a finite world in order to reach the Infinite, modern man brought the infinite down to earth. When the merchant adventurers of the sixteenth century sailed beyond the Straits and faced the western seas, they exulted in the mystery of the world which lay before them. They felt that they were entering an infinite domain whose conquest they sensed as their very destiny.

Modern man began to come into his own at the time of the Renaissance. By the eighteenth century, he dominated the mind and heart of the West. By then Nature had become an infinite womb from whence were born both human personality and human culture. The three together—nature, personality, culture—constituted the whole of being. Follow nature: develop your personality: become cultured! These were the battle cries of modern man. If a thing was natural, it was good. If it furthered personality, it was an absolute. If it was part of our cultural inheritance, it was inviolate.

This unique way of looking at the cosmos lasted until beyond the turn of the twentieth century. By the end of the first World War, however, this vision and the man who sustained it began to give way to a new vision and to a new man. This new man will soon supplant modern man altogether. This new man is Mass Man.

Mass man, says Guardini, rejects the old confidence in and love of nature; he rejects the ideal of a full development of human personality; he is uninterested in the old culture. Man no longer feels any need to refresh himself at that spring of being—the world of nature—which has forever been a sacramental and a balm to the human spirit. Nature—addressed no more in the feminine—has become a cosmic cripple which desperately needs the ministrations of modern science in order that it might be led into the ways of health and even salvation. Nature, therefore, has no value as it is in itself; it exists solely for the sake of its exploitation and "humanization" at the hands of technology. In his most distant dream, mass man sees himself at the center of a world wherein he has conquered the supposedly immutable distinction between Subject and Object, Same and Other, Man and Nature. Mass man dreams of looking out upon a world which is nothing but a mechanized image of himself, a world of mirrors from which an independent nature has vanished into legend and fable. Thus nature either fades away and becomes that last inaccessible residuum lying just beyond the reach of scientific understanding, or nature is admitted within the walls of technology wherein it is symbolized in mathematical formulae. The dizzying consequences of these formulae have thus far defied experience. For the first time in history, man lives within a world he cannot see with his eyes and feel with his hands. But he does not seem to miss the experience! His goal is not experience but power. And this dream is dreamed in the plural, in the collective. The man of the masses sinks himself deeply into the crowd and accepts anonymity as the condition of his very existence. He suspects the idiosyncratic as a gun pointed at his heart. Mass man is man without a personality.

Guardini's study is beyond pessimism and optimism as we understand these concepts in the English-speaking world. Not only does Guardini reject the old gospel of progress, but he insists that there is no chance of grafting the old personal world to the new world of technologized anonymity. The old and new simply have nothing in common. The old aristocratic ideal of the universal man must perforce collapse in a world wherein all effort is cooperative if not absolutely collectivist. The old bourgeois ideal of a full warm life lived within the bosom of the private family cannot co-exist with a new age whose social structure is better symbolized by the factory and the barracks than by the cottage and the castle.

If hope for humanity can be found anywhere within the anonymous world of the masses, it must come—thinks Guardini—from out of the masses themselves. The Christian hope of the future is in a new ethic of power, an ethic that faces—sternly and without pathos—the consequences of man's awesome mastery over nature. Tomorrow's battle for the soul will be fought without that hypocritical tolerance which drained the modern world of honor and clogged the soul with deceit. The old world hoped to retain the values but not the faith of Christ. The new world will be more honest. The battle between Christ and Anti-Christ will be a naked and clean struggle between giants stripped of all finery. Christian Faith will call for an heroism unknown to our fathers, the martyrs of ages past. The Christian of tomorrow will be a man of the masses; he will be conditioned psychologically like his atheist co-workers. His grip on the supernatural will not be buttressed by that natural sense of the divine, that awareness of the numinous in all things, that man has until now felt as he looked out on a world other than himself. Seeking God, the Christian of the future will scan the horizon in vain; nowhere in the new age will he find Him, but only in that love which conquers the world.

It is doubtful whether Guardini's thesis will be accepted fully by all his English-speaking readers. His thesis cuts across the usual division of thinking men into reactionaries and progressives, into those who recoil in horror from the new world and attempt to go back and those who accept the consequences of the present and attempt to forge ahead. According to Guardini the alternatives are neither reaction nor progress: we cannot go back nor can we advance. Man can never retreat in history, but today he is also blocked from advancing into the future. The new age is precisely that—something absolutely new and therefore not a development of what has gone before it.

Some of Guardini's readers, appalled the more by his own prophecy of things to come, will redouble their effort in favor of reaction. Like Chesterton, they will see themselves as members of a band of men who "shall be left defending, not only the incredible...sanities of human life, but something more incredible still, this huge impossible universe which stares us in the face.... We shall look on the impossible grass and the skies with a strange courage. We shall be of those who have seen and yet have believed." Their motto will be the freedom of man against the blind tyranny of history. Others, while accepting Guardini's rejection of any return to the past and to an older world, will bridle at his grim picture of the new age of mass man. Echoing Emmanuel Mounier's *Be Not Afraid*, they will continue to see in human history "A deep continuous impulse driving...from one level to a better...a movement towards the liberation of man." Their motto will be a declaration of faith in the ultimate benevolence of history.

In any event, Guardini's thought is perhaps too revolutionary, too sweeping in its vision and daring in its judgments, to capture with completeness the critical mind. For the uncritical, it is too pitiless.

If he accept or reject, in whole or in part, the thesis of *The End of the Modern World*, the book will nonetheless cauterize the spirit of any man who reads it; it will burn away that sentimentality with which so many today view the advent of the new order, imagining—as they do—that a fully technologized universe can retain every significant cultural and traditional value sustained by the past. Guardini has dispelled the fog of secularization; he has cleared the air; he has shown us rising within our very midst the world which is to come. He offers us Faith, neither in man nor in history, but in God alone and in His Providence.

Frederick D. Wilhelmsen

The first three chapters of this study were composed as a set of lectures which explored the meaning of Pascal's vision of man and the world. My prolonged studies produced an intimacy with the thought of Pascal which indicates that he is related to the modern world in a manner distinctly his own, in a manner proper to one who was both a psychologist and a philosopher of the meaning of Christian existence. He belongs to that company of men who saw the whole situation of the new world which was then coming to be. Whereas his great contemporary and antagonist, Descartes, was completely merged into that shaping world, Pascal surmounts and reaches beyond the modern age. This is true both because Pascal formulated a philosophy and an ethics whose significance is only now being fully revealed and because he assumed a critical attitude toward that newer world.

From Pascal's life and thought emerge questions about the nature of his age and about his engagement with it. What happened to the Western world when the Middle Ages collapsed and a new world came into being? How did Pascal adjust himself to the disappearance of the one and the growth of the other? In attempting to answer these questions, I have sketched with broad strokes the medieval conception of the world; moving then to the vision and temper of modern thought, I have tried to delineate the picture of existence which the latter produced. This task was easily undertaken—as such a task would not have been for men of other periods—because in all crucial respects the modern world has come to an end. Since the spirit of an age becomes wholly clear only when it has begun to vanish from the face of the earth, it has been possible to draw a picture of the modern world without falling victim either in a spirit of admiration or of hatred to the thing represented.

Of itself my work led me into further studies which threw a shaft of light onto the epoch which is coming but is still unknown. It disclosed how deeply penetrating is the change everywhere passing over the world; it intimated the tasks which man will then have to face.

Nothing is said about Pascal in this book. Some might object to a unique study being drawn from meditations which were only intended for university lectures introducing the thought of Pascal. Friends and students urged, however, that my introduction itself could be of some service in book form, and I have taken their advice.

I should like to point out to my readers at the same time that this study is only an attempt to orient oneself within the tangled or fluid situation which still marks our age. Thus the following reflections are marked in many ways by the tentative character of preliminary observations.

I should also like to mention that I have retained the inner form of my original introduction to Pascal, although the manuscript has been intensively rewritten. The reader will not find this work a treatise; rather, it is a series of successive lectures which were offered first during the winter session (1947-48) at Tübingen, then during the summer session (1949) at the University of Munich.

I should also add that the ideas presented in this book are related to those developed in the following studies: *Briefe vom Comer See* (1927), *Welt und Person* (1937) and *Freiheit, Gnade, Schiksal* (1948).

Romano Guardini
Munich, July 1950

***

ACKNOWLEDGMENT

In section two of this book—*Power and Responsibility*—except for a few places where the older translations are more appropriate, the Biblical quotations used in this translation are in the translation of Monsignor Ronald A. Knox, Copyright 1944, 1948 and 1950 Sheed and Ward, Inc., New York. Permission to use the Knox translation was given by His Eminence the Cardinal Archbishop of Westminster.

I.

THE END OF THE MODERN WORLD

A Search for Orientation

THE SENSE OF BEING AND THE WORLD
PICTURE OF THE MIDDLE AGES

[I]

If we are to recapture that vision of the world which medieval man made his own, we must begin with what the Middle Ages had in common with classical antiquity. In neither period can we find the conception which is so familiar to us of an unending space-time relationship. Both ages saw the world and, more significantly, felt it to be a limited frame, a ball [or sphere].

Within this structure, however, there were marked differences between the classical and the medieval views. Classical man never went beyond his world; his feeling for life, his imagination and his vision of existence were one with the limited world he knew. He never asked himself whether or not something might exist beyond his known world. His attitude was born of an unintentional humility, shy of crossing well-marked boundaries, and of a will which was rooted deeply in the classical ethos and kept him within the limits of accepted things. Primarily, classical man felt as he did because he lacked any relation which could transcend his world; such a relation would have been indispensable before he could have experienced any desire to see beyond his universe. To the man of the ancient world, however, the universe itself was the whole of reality. What could classical man have used then as his springboard into transcendence? One might answer: the experience of a Divine Being Who transcended the whole of the limited cosmos, Whose existence and very reality would alter the world outlook of anyone who believed in Him. But classical man never knew such a Being.

From his religious convictions he knew a highest "father of the gods and men," but this father belonged to his own world just as did the vaults of heaven; in truth he was their very spirit. Classical man knew the power of a Fate which commanded his world; he knew of a governing justice and of a reasonable order for all things. These forces, all-powerful though they were, did not stand beyond the world but formed within it its ultimate order.

When he played the role of philosopher the man of classical antiquity tried to conceive of a divine absolute stripped of all imperfection, but even this attempt did not transcend the universe. What is most revealing is the fact that classical man had no desire to transcend his world. Speaking most accurately we must say that classical man *could not* even conceive of a desire to break the limits of his world. To do so those limits must have already been broken. This was simply not the case. Even the pure being of Parmenides, which looks as though it were separated from the concrete world, was itself a principle to which the multiplicity of experience turned as to its ultimate source. The Parmenidean being was a defense against that power so deeply oppressive to the man of Greece, the power of dissolution and corruption. The Good discovered by Plato as the ultimate reality beyond his Ideas was not severed from the world; it remained immanent to it as its very eternity, as a "beyond" within the final whole. The Unmoved Mover of Aristotle, itself immobile, brought about all the change in the world. In final analysis it only had meaning when related to the whole of the eternally changing universe itself. The One of Plotinus, the supreme classical effort to surmount the world of things and men, still stood at the head of an unbroken series with it. The Plotinean One was the spring from which the many flowed by necessity, just as it was the end to which all things returned through purification and love.

Classical man knew nothing of a being existing beyond the world; as a result he was neither able to view nor to shape his world from a vantage point which transcended it. With his feelings and his imagination, in his actions and all his endeavors, he lived within his cosmos. Every project that he undertook, even when he dared to go to the farthest bounds, ran its course within the arc of his world.

One might object that in order to conceive of the universe as a limited whole, the universe must already have been grasped as limited. Such an intuition, so goes the argument, would have had to presuppose the defining boundaries of its world.

This does not, however, hold true for the experience of classical man as far as I can see. His vision resulted from a mental act which sets limits to his being, which fended off the chaotic and the indefinite and which renounced every excess. It also developed from a sense of harmony in which existence was perceived as a beautifully ordered cosmion.

Consequently, classical man did not attempt the comprehension which was so characteristic of medieval man: the world comprehended as a whole within which each individual was assigned a necessary place. Life for classical man remained open and problematic.

This truth is seen most clearly in classical man's religious intuitions and attitudes. He experienced his world itself as divine, divine in the principle which was its inner source and divine in the order and fate which had laid out its roadway. Yet origin, order and fate were themselves part of that world. His world was the All; it was one with existence itself. The world, reality in its fullness, encompassed not merely the empirical and the historical; above all it encompassed the spiritual. The Divine was identified with the primordial, with a mystery which was one with his world. Man was in the universe, but in turn the universe was in him. The experience and affirmation of this truth were the foundations of classical religion.

The multitude of forms and forces within the world manifested the divine, and mythology was born as classical man experienced them. His myths in form and incident symbolized for him the complexity of the universe and of the life of man therein. Because of his own spiritual nature classical man confronted this universe as well as belonging to it. Through his myths classical man found his place in existence. Myth established the unity not of a rational system but of life itself. Forever in flux, the myths constantly assumed new forms as they grew—in the very manner of a living organism—and replaced or melted into one another.

In time these mythological foundations were cut off from classical religious sentiment, as the latter allied itself with the aims of philosophy and ethics. Classical religion still retained the liberal character of its roots, however, changing freely with its particular intellectual affinity. Parmenides, Socrates, Empedocles, the Pythagoreans, Plato, Aristotle, the Stoics, the Plotinians—each thinker, every school—expressed a fresh religious conviction, but always one which was open to new departures. With every new door tried by the spirit of philosophy, the spirit of religion seemed to open onto ever-expanding vistas.

This flexibility and absence of dogmatism also marked Greek scientific thought. The Greek mind was gripped by an endless quest for understanding of the ways of the world. Nothing, however, had been decided conclusively; every question remained open, waiting to be answered further. Every philosophical reflection might contain the answer to life; therefore it could compete with any other possible supposition. Always, however, one had to remain within the limits laid down by the fundamental ethos of the Greek world. These limits could not be transgressed, and the trials of

Anaxagoras and of Socrates attest to the strength of this prohibition. Thus the Greek searched and hunted for the truth; he experimented with all hypotheses. At the end of his epoch, he had gathered up not only a full body of knowledge but also a typology for every possible position and conclusion in philosophy.

This same cast of mind penetrated Greek social and political life. The several city states of Greece gave birth to a variety of political forms, each state developing independently of its neighbors and according to those geographical conditions and traditional assumptions which were proper to itself. Political ambition within and conflict among the many states was taken as the normal condition of historic life. Thus the individual was absorbed by his particular community. The increasing rivalries among the city states furthered the growth of independent political forms, each of which was rooted deeply in an historic spirit of that people. This profuse flowering of political life, however, swiftly burned itself out in internecine struggles. An attempt to unify the Hellenic peoples into a single political state could not succeed because the Greek in the depths of his soul did not want a unified polity, not even when unity offered the only promise of a continued historic existence. The Greeks chose to tear themselves asunder in senseless wars until the half-barbaric Macedonians forced upon them an artificial kind of unity which violated their unique way of life. Such political blindness points up an essential weakness in the Greek ethos which is often overlooked by its admirers.

We could multiply the instances from the Greek

world in which this picture returns again and again. It was a world built by men who rooted themselves in being as they knew it, by men who had a primitive yet never faltering intuition into the things that are; it was the result of a fruitful as well as a dangerous liberality in the conduct of private and social life.

We might be tempted to speak of one ancient effort which violated the spirit of Greek liberalism and which attempted to organize all life into a unified whole: the Roman State. It is certain that Rome did attempt to build the *orbis terrarum*. The Roman spirit was realistic and suspicious of the theoretical, hostile to the metaphysical. Despite all its harshness when confronted with the exigencies of political existence, however, it looked upon life itself with an extreme liberality. The spirit of tolerance found in the classic Greek world was not abolished by the Roman Empire.

[II]

The Middle Ages transformed radically man's sense of existence and his vision of the world. Medieval man centered his faith in Revelation as it had been enshrined in Scripture, in that Revelation which affirmed the existence of a God Who holds His Being separate and beyond the world. Since He creates and sustains all things in being and fills them with His Presence God is in His world, but He does not belong to the world because He is its Sovereign. The independence of God is fixed in the absoluteness of His

Being and in the purity of His Personality. An irreducibly personal God can never be merged with any universe; He exists solely in Himself, Lord of His Being. Loving the world He depends in no sense upon it. The mythical deities of classical antiquity, however, had to stand or fall with their worldly kingdoms. The absolute essences of ancient philosophy were enmeshed forever within the totality of being to which they gave stability and eternity. But the Christian God needs no world in order that He might be; subsisting alone He is sufficient unto Himself.

The doctrine of creation most decisively reveals the power of God, the Infinite Sovereign. The world was created out of nothing by the freedom of the Almighty Whose commanding Word gives to all things being and nature; of itself that world lacks any trace of internal necessity or external possibility. This created universe is found only in the Bible. Elsewhere the origin of the universe was always thought to have been mythical; either some formless chaos had evolved into the world or some divine power had fashioned it from an equally formless chaos. The Revelation of Scripture contradicted all such myth: the world is created by a God Who does not have to create in order that He might be, nor does He need the elements of the world in order that He might create.

Christian Faith meant trust in and obedience to God's Revelation to man. It also meant that man must confront and answer His Call, which alone gives meaning to finite personality. Finally, it meant that man must turn toward the Lord as toward his final end.

In this Faith the world was born afresh, but it was born neither of mythology nor of philosophy. The mythical bonds which had chained man to the universe were destroyed. A new freedom dawned in history for the human spirit. Sundered now from the world, man was able for the first time to face all things from a new plane, from a vantage point which depended neither upon intellectual superiority nor cultural attainment. Thereupon was wrought a transfiguration of being utterly impossible for the old pagan world.

Deeply significant for the new religious outlook of medieval man was the influx of the Germanic spirit. The religious bent of the Nordic myths, the restlessness of the migrating peoples and the armed marches of the Germanic tribes revealed a new spirit which burst everywhere into history like a spear thrust into the infinite. This mobile and nervous soul worked itself into the Christian affirmation. There it grew mightily. In its fullness it produced that immense medieval drive which aimed at cracking the boundaries of the world.

This medieval impatience with all limitations cannot be explained, however, simply in terms of the Christian view of man and his relationship to God. Nothing akin to the medieval drive can be found in the first centuries of the Faith, when the classical sense of limitation still retained its hold on Christian man. Although he experienced transcendence, he experienced it only as an inner freedom from the world and as a personal responsibility for his own life, a responsibility transcending the demands and service of society. Only after the Germanic ferment has quickened the European world throughout the course and aftermath of migrations was man's relation to God freed from the boundaries fixed by antiquity. Only then did man scale the barriers of the world and reach into the infinite that he might embrace the Godhead and return from Him to make all things new.

The Germanic longing to embrace the whole of being was one with the drive for transcendence. The Germanic spirit wished to surround the world in order to penetrate it completely. This passion both to embrace and to enter deeply the full sweep of existence explains the new vision of the world fashioned by medieval man. We shall now study from several points of view this new world in both its cosmological and existential dimensions.

The external world was pictured according to the old Ptolemaic theory, but the theory itself was more firmly conceived than it had been by the ancients. Created and governed in the whole of its being and charged with symbols bearing both metaphysical and religious value, the cosmos gained an entirely new character. The universe of Ptolemy was seen now illuminated by the biblical doctrines of the sovereignty, the creativity and the government of God, the Archetype of all things.

The whole of the cosmos appeared as a series of concentric spheres. At the center was the sphere of the earth. Around the earth circled the other spheres, enormous and incorruptible in substance, to each of which was attached one of the planets and lastly the stars. (Neither classical nor medieval man understood the laws of gravitation; therefore neither could conceive of the free movement of bodies in space.) There were nine spheres with that most distant from the earth, the *primum mobile,* closing in the universe. Beyond this last sphere extended the Empyrean, burning and luminous. Man could not "really" include the Empyrean in his vision of the world, however, because the whole of created being was held within that world. In fact the Empyrean rendered his world finite, both bordering upon it and enclosing it as it did. Here the astronomical representation mingled with the religious picture, or more accurately with a "picture" created by religious vision. As such it could not be represented at all, for the Empyrean was the place of God, and man would not presume to "see" either God or His "place." In this way medieval man saw his world, however, because it was in part a religious vision; it had to retain a place for God.

If the Empyrean, "the Place of God," extended beyond the world and transcended all things, there had to be a "counter-place," an absolute center for the cosmos. This opposite place was the middle of the earth. At that center cosmology was linked with religious vision in two ways: negatively, the counterplace took color from the classic underworld as a kingdom of doom and horror, as the deeps of the world where God was contradicted, as the Hell of Dante's *Divine Comedy;* affirmatively, the counterplace was stripped of its spatial and cosmic dimensions to become the inner man, the "sphere" of heart and soul.

It became clear to medieval man when he turned his spirit in upon itself, when he descended to the core of his soul, that he reached a frontier of "inner finiteness." Beyond it was the dwelling place of God again, but it was just as inconceivable as was the great expanse of transcendence where dwelt the Lord. To maintain his total cosmology, medieval man had to allow his spirit to think of "something" lying beyond the innermost side of that frontier of "inner finiteness"—a not-something and yet a something—the "place of God," Who has crossed over and come into the world, into man's soul as Immanence. There also "lived" God. In the Empyrean, however, God reigned publicly as the high Lord of all things; within the depths of the human soul He dwelt inwardly and privately. Both were "places" transcending the two farthest poles of reality: the first, lying beyond the uttermost sphere of creation; the second, lying buried to the "other side" of the inmost core of the soul of man.

Between these extreme points floated the world. As a whole and in each of its parts the world was the portrait of God; that is, the rank and excellence of every created being was determined by the degree to which it bore within itself the stamp of God's image. A vast hierarchy of being—the non-living, the plants and the animals—was formed by the interrelations of the many things found in these realms of essence. At the highest, man in his rational-spiritual life was enabled to gather all lesser things into a unity unknown to the ancients and true to the revealed creation of God, into the unity of the macrocosm in all its ranks and degrees, in the fullness of its meaning.

Modern astronomy has refuted this total construction of the medieval genius which gave expression to reality as it is directly grasped by the human eye and consciousness. For this very reason the theory has a most penetrating symbolic power in human thought. Even today its existential[1] validity cannot be denied, while its influence upon the ways of medieval man was profound.

Again we must insist that the utterly crucial truth for medieval man was the fact of Divine Revelation. Above and beyond everything given man in this world Revelation was the absolute fulcrum. Set forth within the dogma of the Church, Revelation was accepted upon faith by the individual. From one point of view the Church bound and limited man by its authority; from another point of view the Church made it possible for man to surmount his world. She gave a vision which of itself was vast and liberating in scope. Revealed truth was conceptualized by means of a delicate logic which distinguished and then united all of reality. The theological system erected upon these foundations unfolded itself as a great synthesis. In the modern sense of the term, however, scientific explanation was almost unknown. The one point of departure for science in the medieval intellectual synthesis was authority, that of antiquity and especially the work of Aristotle. The relation between medieval and classical thought was intrinsically organic, a relation having little in common with the attitudes toward classicism displayed by the mind of the Renaissance. The latter was critical and revolutionary; the Renaissance used its fidelity to the classical as a tool with which it cut itself away from Revelation and ecclesiastical authority. By contrast, the Middle Ages had established a relationship with antiquity which although seeming naive was constructive. Viewing classical literature as a direct expression of natural truth, the Middle Ages simply developed and amplified its content.

By the closing years of the twelfth and the beginning of the thirteenth centuries, however, contradictions between classicism and Revelation were strongly experienced by the medieval mind. These first suspicions soon disappeared, and medieval man simply accepted the world of ancient philosophy as a truth given *per se* to the intelligence. That world was taken to be as natural a servant to Revelation as was nature itself; it was, so to speak, taken as a "second degree" nature. When Dante referred to Christ as *somme Giove*, he did exactly what the liturgy does when it sees Christ as the *sol salutis*. This spirit was altogether different, however, from that of the Renaissance scholars when they gave Christian figures names taken from the gods of antiquity. The latter practice was a sign either of confusion or of inner skepticism. The former was an expression of conviction; the world was the property of those who believed in its Creator. Medieval exegesis was bent on reconciling both the conflicts found among the classical authorities themselves and the differences between their thought and Revelation.

This drive for reconciliation is crystallized in the *Summae*[2] which united theology and philosophy, sociology and morality. Impressive works of art in themselves, the *Summae* seem strangely foreign to modern man until he discovers the key to medieval efforts; namely, that medieval man neither wished to explore the mysteries of the world empirically nor did he want to illuminate them by a rational methodology. He was interested in building his world out of the content of Revelation and upon the principles and insights of classical philosophy. The *Summae* are that world as it was erected by the human mind. They are a world in which vast differences were fused into a powerful synthesis; they can be compared with the medieval cathedral in which every form and artifact— even the simplest materials of construction—were given a symbolic value which made possible a life and a sense of being integrally religious in nature.

The above analysis has been heightened in effect and must not be misunderstood. We do not mean to say that the Middle Ages did nothing except work over the ancient intellectual ideas; we do not mean to say that it was not engaged in a most profound intellectual effort. That would be to grossly oversimplify. In truth the classical view of the world yielded a rich storehouse for mastery by the medieval mind, offering it a genuine intellectual advance. Even when classic thought had been absorbed by the medieval world at large, it was worked over again and expanded by each medieval scholar independently. As well, the medieval thinker went directly to the world of existing things, to those things which he experienced immediately in sensation; he reflected upon their essences and status within the interdependent ordering of creation. From those reflections medieval man garnered a wisdom which even today has its value. Medieval anthropology, for example, in both principle and application, is superior to its modern counterpart. In morality and moral attitude, medieval life had a firmer yet richer hold on reality than is possible for modern man; it also made possible a fuller perfecting of human nature. In social philosophy and jurisprudence, medieval thought encompassed and ordered its concrete cultural situation to its own time, yet it offers insights which have basic validity for man at any time.

What medieval man lacked was any desire for exact, empirical knowledge of reality, and he did run the risk of merely repeating the classical authorities under whose discipline he had placed himself. It cannot be denied, however, that he had the opportunity to develop an intellectual synthesis completely beyond the scope of modern individualism. We grasp this difference even more clearly and forcefully when we remember that the medieval synthesis was the work not only of individuals, but also of an interplay between school and tradition. This corporate endeavor allowed medieval man to refine and deepen his earliest visions and to expand them to their fullest.

Society itself was governed by two great ideas:

Church and Empire as incarnated in the persons of the Pope and the Emperor. Both areas of society were rooted in the supernatural, both were sanctified by divine grace, both were hallowed by investiture, both were lifted above all other things. From on high they governed together the world of Christian life. The Pope wore the triple tiara and held the keys of St. Peter in his hand; the Emperor was clothed with the blue, star-spangled robe which represented the arc of the heavens and held a scepter in his hand, the imperial globe as sign of the world. All the orders of society were marshaled around these fixed centers of authority; all human powers from the lowest to the highest echelons were gathered before them. From the most humble to the most exalted, whether of symbol, rank or function, the whole rhythm of life pointed to those centers.

Above the orders of Church and Empire in which the government of the entire world centered hovered the heavenly ranks of purely spiritual beings, the angels. These angelic choirs and those earthly orders harmonized with one another in a mighty host of correspondences, in a magnificent unity, in a sweeping hierarchy.

The very history of medieval Christendom, however, was to be fixed by the powerful tensions which threatened the unity of Church and Empire. The mounting struggle between Pope and Emperor was a profounder one than it seems at first glance. The struggle had little to do with the mere externals of political power; its roots lay much deeper. It was a struggle over the unity of existence itself. Assisted by the champions of feudal rights, the Emperors attempted to bend the Church to their will. Under the stress of early migrations the Empire had succeeded in its rivalry with the Church, allowing it to claim its superiority of office on spiritual grounds alone. In time the Popes demanded that the throne of the Emperor should be subject to Papal authority. Under Gregory VII and Innocent III, the Papacy did succeed in establishing that unity of all existence which haunted the medieval mind as its very dream. Born from this conflict and bred of this dream was a third medieval theory: it concluded that the two principles of Church and State were united only through the fact that both derived their power and their office from the high authority of God Himself. Behind every such attempt at unity we find the same intention. Human life in the total sweep of its existence and in all its works must be founded upon and ordered by the transcendent sublimity of the Lord.

The orders of Church and State with the orders of the angels above them gathered all things into an architectonic unity. In the successiveness of history, as well, was seen another unity, which was expressed in the theory of world periods. The theory rested upon the Old Testament message of Daniel, 7-12, and was fully developed by St. Augustine in the *De Civitate Dei.*[3]

The Middle Ages accepted the Augustinian theory of history even as it developed Augustine's teaching. The theory reinforced the basic medieval conviction that the universe was a rather large yet limited whole. Revelation again opened the eyes of the faithful here and gave them a point of view which elevated them above the boundaries given to life by immediate sensation. The world, time, history had begun with Creation; they reached apotheosis in the Incarnation of the Son of God—"the Fullness of Time"—and all shall end with the destruction of the world and the Last Judgment. Between the Creation and the End of Things, history itself was divided into epochs of time which were paralleled by the Days of Creation themselves. The birth of Christ began our own time which itself is the last of all the ages, an age filled with hope for the Second Coming and with expectations of Judgment.

These speculations were amplified theoretically in a number of works, such as Bonaventure's *Work of the Six Days.* Hexameral thought was expounded more concretely in a host of chronicles in which the matter of Creation itself was embellished by recording all the great deeds of history which the chronicler could muster from the past up to his own lifetime. This practice gave rise to a definite attitude toward the events of history which was peculiarly medieval. The historical event was framed and fixed in its own place in time by situating it between a definite beginning and a decisive end. It followed that the "now" of existence stood out with a clear-cut fullness of meaning; each moment of time was etched against the sweeping panorama of history. Each present moment gained its uniqueness from the impact of the Incarnation which marked the piercing of time itself by eternity. Of greater significance, each present moment of existence became an historic center, for each was given the burden of choice in that crucial and irreducible drama that is one with existence itself.

The most complete ordering of medieval life was found in its religious point of view and practice, in its Christian "cult." Expressed by myriad symbolic forms, that cult affirmed repeatedly the eternal significance of salvation for every moment in human life. In the dimension of space, that cult found expression in medieval architecture, especially in the cathedral or episcopal chair which dominated all other churches in the diocese. These churches in their turn carried forward the blessed work, sanctifying space itself by spreading cemeteries, chapels and wayside crosses over the land. The very land became hallowed by the presence of the Church at large. Each church building itself through the supernatural rite of consecration symbolized and enfolded the whole of Creation. Every part of a church building from the direction of its main axis to its most minute appointments was invested with a divine meaning which fused the cosmic picture of the world with the course of sacred history into a symbolic whole. The countless figures of the saints and the stories of salvation were everywhere carved in wood, emblazoned in color and glorified by the art of stained glass. In the very fullness of its being the world of the spirit stood before the eyes of the people.

This same sacred world was evoked by the seasons of the ecclesiastical year and by the constant succession of days made holy by the Church. The rotation

of the sun was linked by the Church with the sacred
rhythm proper to its own life; to the cycle of the seasons and of annual change, it joined the life of
Christ—*sol salutis*. Thus the Church moved forward
gathering all things into an inexhaustible unity. The
world of time was further enriched in spirit when
the Church added the feasts of the saints—whose
lives dramatized the work of salvation—to the feasts
celebrating the life of Christ Himself. Re-enacted
year in year out in the liturgy of each and every
church in Christendom, this symbolic rendering of
time became the very rhythm of temporal life. Every
event of life for a man or for his family—birth, marriage, death, labor and rest, the advent of the
seasons, the passing of the weeks, the deeds of the
day—each of them breathed the rhythm of the
ecclesiastical year. That rhythm had become one
with the single moment and with the span of man's
life even to his last extremity.

As well as expressing itself in space and time
Christian cult brought to literature a sacred symbolism. The highest and most authoritative
literary expression was found in the pontificals
and rituals, in the Mass books and breviaries. For
the people Christian cult was embodied in the
widely popular "house books" of the *Legenda Aurea*
[or *The Golden Legends*].

Universal in scope the symbolism created by the
Christian cult of medieval man thus covered and permeated the whole of being. Life was seen as a rich and
diversified hierarchy; every class in society and all

things in nature had their beginning and their end, their origin and their fulfillment, their departure and their return. Every least and greatest thing in being was led back to its source in eternity.

Dante's *Divine Comedy* is perhaps the most powerful embodiment of this medieval sense of the unity of all things in being. Written at the end of the high Middle Ages, at the very moment when the medieval spirit had begun to ebb, the *Divine Comedy* stands alone. The medieval drama seen against the background of impending darkness was loved the more by Dante. In his pages it shines with a transfigured beauty.

[III]

Unless we free ourselves of the evaluations made by the minds of the Renaissance and the Enlightenment we cannot really understand the Middle Ages. The judgments then leveled were made under the pressure of a polemic which has succeeded in distorting the truth even to our own day. Equally distorted was the glorified Middle Ages of the Romantics who gave the period a frankly "canonical" character it never possessed. The excessive enthusiasm of the Romantics has prevented many a man from arriving at a balanced view of medieval Christendom.

From our present standpoint the Middle Ages can readily be turned into a mixture of primitive simplicity and fantastic imagination, into a fusion of naked force and base servility. But this picture has nothing to do with historical truth. There is only one standard by which any epoch can be fairly judged: in view of its own peculiar circumstances, to what extent did it allow for the development of human dignity? The medieval achievement was so magnificent that it stands with the loftiest moments of human history.

The Middle Ages were filled with a sense of religion which was as deep as it was rich, as strong as it was delicate, as firm in its grasp of principles as it was original and fertile in their concrete expression. From cloister and monastery there shone a religious light whose strength cannot be overestimated. We cannot exaggerate the impact which was made upon the corporate consciousness by the ever-fresh stream of worshippers, penitents and mystics which poured forth from the springs of medieval piety. From all these sources of faith tumbled the waters of religious experience, wisdom and certitude which constantly freshened and quickened every class and degree of society.

Medieval man thirsted for the truth. No other society, with the possible exception of that which bore the culture of classical China, has invested the man of learning with the dignity and importance given him by the Middle Ages. The medieval passion for understanding, however, had nothing in common with our modern enthusiasm for the techniques of scientific investigation. Medieval man was interested neither in pursuing nature and history empirically nor in mastering reality theoretically. He chose to plunge into truth by way of meditation; then he drew from his meditations the spiritual laws governing all reality.

The roots for all truths were given him by authority: the roots of divine truth by Scripture and the Church; of natural truth by the thought of antiquity. These foundations for religious and natural truth were painstakingly penetrated, and when fully understood they acted as the bases for interpreting whatever truths could be grasped through immediate experience. From this fusion of natural and supernatural truths, there grew a new and deeper understanding of the world and of all reality. The ideal underlying a process of strict experimentation or, as we would term it, scientific investigation was foreign to the Middle Ages. Whenever it did appear it was sensed to be something alien, even dangerous. It is significant that Albert the Great, although canonized a saint, became a magician in medieval story and legend.

The medieval conception of the world also gave birth to an elemental powerful feeling for the symbolic value of existence itself. Medieval man saw symbols everywhere. He did not look upon reality in terms of energy, the elements, or physical laws; he saw things in terms of form. The forms he saw not only had their own meaning, but they pointed also to something higher, ultimately to the things of eternity, to the Most High Himself, to God. All forms became symbols of the divine. They came down from above, appearing as it were "from their own other side." These symbolic forms were found in Christian cult and in the arts, in the customs and speech of the people and in communal life. Indeed they influenced the work of the intellect to such an extent that one often feels the intellectual explanation of a phenomenon, or the elaboration of a theory, was guided less by the matter at hand than by a number-symbolism intrinsic to the formal structure of the mind itself. [4]

The philosophical-theological *Summae* were more than a systematic attempt to determine what being must "be"; they were an attempt to determine what being must "mean." The meaning expressed in the *Summae* arose not alone from its content; it arose equally from the very mode of statement and amplification. This fact reveals a fourth component in the basic medieval drive—the artistic. As used in molding and shaping the thought of the *Summae*, artistic form was not mere rhetorical adornment; it was not merely a desirable—in final analysis an unessential—means of expression; it was the "how" used to express the really essential "what." The medieval passion for truth was so intense that it was bound up inextricably with a will to fashion and form all things. Thus the very construction of a *quaestio* as it was used to pose a problem guaranteed clarity of investigation, an adequate weighing of pro and con and of the relations between the problem and previous thought. To the *quaestio* was given a formal aesthetic value comparable with that of a sonnet or a fugue. A *quaestio* was not simply a medium by which truth could be read by the mind understanding it; it was a truth formed and shaped by mind to speak to mind. Artistic form then embodied another yet certain truth about the world. It was simply the truth that reality itself was ordered harmoniously in being, that it could be formed and fashioned by the artistic genius of man. A complete *Summa* in its articles, its questions and its parts was a structured unity within which the human spirit could linger and take its repose. A *Summa* was not only a book of science; it was a "space," vast in its ontology— deep and ordered—wherein the human spirit found its proper place and exercised that self-discipline necessary to experience security.

It is cheap and false to condemn the medieval use of authority as "slavery." Modern man makes this judgment not merely because he enjoys the discovery of autonomous investigation but because he resents the Middle Ages. His resentment is born of the realization that his own age has made revolution a perpetual institution. But authority is needed not only by the childish but also in the life of every man, even the most mature. Integral to the full grandeur of human dignity, authority is not merely the refuge of the weak; its destruction always breeds its burlesque—force.

As long as medieval man was gripped by his own vision of existence, as long as he heard its music sounding in the depths of his heart, he never experienced authority as shackling. It was a bridge leading to the absolute; it was the flag of the world. Authority provided medieval man with the opportunity to construct an order whose magnificence of form, intensity of manner and richness of life were such that he would have judged our world as paltry.

NOTES

1. Guardini uses the term "existential" in its current philosophical sense. "Existential," therefore, does not mean that which exists objectively in independence of the act of knowledge; "existential" means "man-in-his-world"; that is, "existential" means man in his total being as he confronts his universe with his senses, his heart, his soul and his intelligence. —Ed.

2. Guardini uses *Summae* (and *Summa*, later) in a generic sense, not in specific reference to one medieval thinker.

3. Guardini is referring to the teaching in Daniel about the Four Realms of the World—Assyria, Persia, Macedonia and Rome; he next refers to St. Augustine's doctrine of the Six Ages of the World, the last age of which corresponded in medieval theory to the Last Realm in Daniel. —Ed.

4. *E.g.*, the Pythagorean number theory.—Ed.

CHAPTER TWO

THE BIRTH OF THE MODERN WORLD

[I]

The medieval picture of the world along with the cultural order which it supported began to dissolve during the fourteenth century. The process of dissolution continued throughout the fifteenth and sixteenth centuries. By the seventeenth century it was complete, and a new picture of reality dawned clearly and distinctly over Europe.

In order to understand that change we must examine again the many things that are the life of a civilization and which feed the roots of its corporate activities. We cannot look for a particular cause of this transformation, any more than we could in our study of the birth of the Middle Ages. No single cause flows through a new world to determine and shape it in its entirety. Rather, we again confront man as he faced, experienced, understood and grappled with the sweep of being.

It is best to start with the appearance of modern science. We have seen that the medieval mind saw science as an activity in which the scholar immersed himself in the authoritative sources of truth. This attitude of mind had begun to decline as early as the late fourteenth century; it was further weakened during the fifteenth. Man's passion for knowledge began to lead him away from authority, pointing him directly toward real things. He chose to probe things with his own intelligence and to reach established judgments which were independent of any pattern first laid down by authority.

In this new thirst for an independent knowledge man looked first to nature. In doing so he gave birth to the modern preoccupation with experiment and rational theory in the physical sciences. He also began that critique of tradition by which the humanists insisted upon writing history merely from source materials. Similarly in probing the life of society he developed the disciplines of state law and jurisprudence. In short, he discovered that the new science had gained a nature of its own as an autonomous cultural process. Severed from the older religious unity of life and work, science stood alone and at one with its essence.

Corresponding changes worked their way into economic life even earlier than the preceding changes; in Italy as early as the late thirteenth century. Previously, a man's livelihood had been linked with his status in life and governed both by guild regulations and by the canonical rules against interest which made economic speculation impossible. The new spirit had brought new methods which increased the production and distribution of goods to an unprecedented degree. The older traditional ordering of society was cracked by the simple possession of things. Offices and positions of rank hitherto restricted to privilege were now thrown open to almost anyone. A broader and more independent culture was born and bred upon an economics which adhered only to its own strict laws.

The older society had been supported in its basic norms and cultural order by the art of politics, even when politics exerted itself in the struggle for the fruits of sheer power. Although shot through with injustice and crime, political life during the Middle Ages had been fitted to the moral and religious obligations owed to the Empire and the Church, those twin symbols for the eternal laws laid down by the Will of God. Political goals were subordinated by the felt need to conform to the Divine Will; an injustice was committed only with a bad conscience. With the advent of the modern world the political goal became an end in itself.

Indeed the modern world has increasingly seen political activities as autonomous. Not only practically but also theoretically the acquiring, maintaining and exercise of power admitted every possible means. Politics was become a law unto itself. Injustice at the service of the political was committed not only without bad conscience, but even from a certain sense of "duty." Machiavelli was the first to express this independent "morality" in the political realm; others were to follow him. Thomas Hobbes, Pascal's contemporary, built his theory of the state upon the assertion that it should be absolute master and judge of human life; life itself he reduced to a mere struggle between man and man.

Those theoretical speculations found ample support in the practical order in the endless wars being waged everywhere between those independent states and principalities from which the modern national states were gradually born. As the peoples of Europe became conscious of their own corporate lives and missions, the vigor of nationalism asserted itself. In doing so it destroyed the old social order. The new politics was as much an instrument as a result of these historic changes.

As radically as with the social and political, man's cosmological picture of the world was altered. Although seen as a whole and limited in size and finite in extension, the finiteness of the world pictured by the older theory was balanced, so to speak, by an infinity in depth. This it gained by the symbolic meaning which shone through the whole of reality. The eternal exemplar of the world was the Logos; every part of the world was a manifestation of this inexhaustible source. Each distinct thing in being was both itself and a related part of a symbolic hierarchy which linked all things in a rich and diversified unity. The angels and the saints in eternity, the stars in the heavens, the objects of nature, man and his soul, human society—in its many levels and in all its functions—appeared as a harmony whose meaning was eternal. History too was fixed, even in the ebb and flow of its many epochs between the absolute beginning, Creation, and the final end, Judgment. The great act in this drama, the historic era, was linked with every other era; within each age every event had its own meaning and multiple relations.

As man discovered that the universe extended farther than he had imagined in every direction, these contours were broken. The old passion for a universe limited in structure, the old desire for a world in which life was directed and channeled, disappeared. Man began to feel that expansion itself was a liberation. Astronomy had discovered that the earth rotated around the sun; no longer could the earth be the center of the universe. In his turbulent writings Giordano Bruno announced his philosophy of an infinity of unending universes. The belief that our world had its unique significance was thrown into question.

The effects of the new astronomy, so immense in themselves, fitted well with the achievements made by the other sciences of nature. Together they furnished the aspiring mind with the conclusion that a world of fantasies had been swept away. Man had finally broken through the veil to see a new world conforming in very truth with reality itself.

Similar currents moved in the discipline of historical research. The absolute beginning and end affirmed for history by Scripture was viewed with a marked skepticism. History seemed to stretch into a distant past hitherto undreamed of; it seemed to reach into a future of dimly distant tomorrows. Studies of source materials, monuments and antiquities unearthed a staggering past littered with ruin yet swarming with facts. Historical causality and new insights into the nature of historical existence raised fresh problems about the relations between historic facts. The single historical event lost its unique significance under the immense weight of historical facts and under the impact of the new conviction that time was unlimited. The multiplicity of historic phenomena allowed a unique importance to no one event; rather all events were viewed as having an indifferent significance and value. As the old sense of limitation was sundered man lost that value given those unique historical "moments" wherein the medieval belief in order had reposed. Gone was the beginning and the end, the limit and the center. The concept of hierarchy faded; with it disappeared not only all related convictions about the nature of culture but also its many symbolic accretions. The new world seemed a fabric woven of innumerable parts, a fabric which expanded in all directions. Even as this new world view affirmed a freedom of space it denied to human existence its own proper place. While gaining infinite scope for movement man lost his own position in the realm of being.

This sense of infinity granted first to the spaces of the universe was soon conferred upon the earth itself. Previously, man had been content to move throughout well-known lands which had been often traveled, whose breadth and boundaries had been delineated. But now he felt no longer that the unknown areas of the earth were occult or forbidden to him. For Dante, Ulysses had been guilty of a crime and a transgression when he sailed beyond the pillars of Gibraltar into open sea. His act led to his destruction. For the new man of the modern age the unexplored regions of his world were a challenge to meet and conquer. Within himself he heard the call to venture over what seemed an endless earth, to make himself its master.

At the same time was born the modern consciousness of man's own personality. Man began to find his
own individuality an absorbing object for study, for
introspection and psychological analysis. The extraordinary in human life, the dignity of man at the height
of personal development, both were seen with a new
awareness. Genius became the most important measure of human value. Genius was identified by analogy
with a universe now expanding to infinity, with a history now without limits. Genius became the standard
for all human judgments.

The experience of modern man then allowed him
movement in two directions. With freedom or liberty
of personal action the self-governing, creatively daring
individual seemed a man carried forward by his own
self-mastered genius. Thus he was led toward his destiny by fortune to be crowned in the end by fame and
glory. This positive experience, however, was coun-
tered by man's loss of his objective sense of belonging
to existence. With the breakdown of the old world picture, man came to feel now only that he had been
placed in a life of strange contradictions but also that
his very existence was threatened. Modern man awoke
to that anxiety which menaces him to this day, an anxiety never found in the medieval world. Medieval man
did experience anxieties; that experience is one with
human nature. Indeed man has always known anxiety,
and even if science and technology succeed in giving
him the appearance of security he will continue to
know anxiety. But the causes and the nature of anxiety
differ with differing times. Medieval anxiety resulted

from the tensions experienced by the soul which although set in a limited universe—one controlled strictly in direction and scope of movement—was bent upon leaping into infinity. Yet medieval tensions were resolved as the soul achieved an ever new and greater transcendence. Modern anxiety, by contrast, arises from man's deep-seated consciousness that he lacks either a "real" or a symbolic place in reality. In spite of his actual position on earth he is a being without security. The very needs of man's senses are left unsatisfied, since he has ceased to experience a world which guarantees him a place in the total scheme of existence.

The new picture of reality was dominated by a number of conceptions, the most important of which was the modern view of "Nature." It had come to signify whatever was given immediately to the mind and sensibilities of man. It was all those things which existed in the world prior to anything man did to them; it was also the sum total of energy, matter, essences and natural laws. Thus "Nature" was readily made a matter of value in itself. It became the norm which guided man in action and in reason toward whatever was right or healthful or perfect. The constant norm was simply the "natural." From this attitude grew a new ethic; the man who was morally good was the "natural" man; so too was the "natural" society or form of government or manner of education or way of life. From the sixteenth to the twentieth century we find this pervasive concept in many guises: in the *honnête homme* of the sixteenth and seventeenth centuries, in the "natural" man of Rousseau, in the rationalism of the Enlightenment, in the "natural" beauty invoked by neoclassicism.

Nature in short signified and determined a something final beyond which it was impossible to venture. Everything derived from the concept of Nature was understood to be an absolute; whatever could be made to conform with Nature was justified by its very conformity. Yet the conception did not allow that Nature could be understood *qua* Nature. On the contrary, Nature contained within itself the mystery of the primitive origin and end of all things. She was "Divine," an object for religious worship; she was praised as creative, wise, benevolent; she was "Mother Nature" to whose truth men surrendered themselves unconditionally. The Natural had become the Holy and the Good.

A sublime expression of this religious emotion is found in Goethe's fragment, "Nature," which was written in 1782 for the *Tiefurtur Journal*:

Nature! We are surrounded and embraced by her. We are without power to rise out of her and without power to plunge deeper into her. She takes us without our leave and with no warning brings us into the circle of her dance, and she moves forward with us until exhausted, we fall from her arms.

She creates eternally new forms; what is, was not before; what was, never returns. All is new and yet everything is old.

We live in her center and are strangers to her. She converses with us endlessly and she does not reveal her secrets to us. We try to submit her to our wishes and we have no power over her.

She, the Mother, lives only in innocent children, but—their mother—where is she? She is the only Artist and she fashions the most simple matter to the most subtle and lofty contrasts; with no sign of exertion she raises matter to the highest perfection, even the most exquisite distinctness, and her work is forever clothed in softness and executed with ease. Each of her children is unique in being; each of her appearances is alone in meaning and yet together they form but one.... She has reasoned and she continues to meditate, but never as a man meditates, but rather as Nature Herself. She holds within her being a unique and embracing tenderness which no amount of observation can steal from her.

From nothing she showers forth her children, and she does not tell them from whence they come nor where they go. It is theirs only to run through life; she knows the direction.

Everything is present within her. She does not know the past and the future. The present only is her eternity. She is benevolent, and I praise her in all her works. She is wise and silent. No man tears an explanation from her body nor bribes from her secrets that she does not freely give. She is crafty, but to a good end, and it is best not to be aware of her cunning.

She put me here; she will lead me away. I place my trust in her. She may dispose of me as she wills. She will never hate her work. I spoke noth-

ing of her. Whatever is true and whatever false
has been spoken by her. All guilt is hers; all merit
is hers.

Such a modern experience of nature was linked
with the ancient classic experience. The classical
awareness of nature is above all a perennially valid
affirmation for that human life which is lived as it
ought to be lived; it was not a peculiar awareness
which occurred in the past of history and disappeared.
When we place the term "classical" within a cultural
setting we have a concept which fits the nature of
man; likewise we can fit the term "natural" to man. But
the modern world affirmed neither nature nor classicism as the Middle Ages had done. For medieval man
nature was the creation of God; classicism was a foreshadowing of Revelation. For modern man both
nature and classicism became means for severing existence from Revelation. Revelation had become empty
of meaning and hostile to life.[1]

Although man is intrinsically bound to nature in
both body and spirit, as soon as he disposes of nature
by coming to know nature he rises out of his natural
milieu. He then places nature opposite himself as
something completely "other." In the process of sepa-
rating himself from nature modern man underwent
that second experience crucial for understanding the
import of modern life. He underwent the experience
of subjectivity.

The modern concept of the subjective is as foreign
to the medieval consciousness as is that of nature.

Seeing nature as the sum, the ordering, and the unity of all things, medieval man could not conceive of nature as an autonomous All. Nature was the Work of the Sovereign God. Man was the subject, being of the order of nature, was first the creature of God and the steward of His Will. With the new consciousness of self, however, which arose late in the Middle Ages and especially in the Renaissance, man became important to himself. The "I"—particularly the "I" of the extraordinary, of genius—became the measure by which all human life was judged.

Subjectivity revealed itself most distinctly in the concept of "personality." Conceived as that which most expressed the human, as flowering from roots intrinsic to itself, as shaped in its destiny through its own initiative, personality became—just as Nature had—something primary and absolute which could not be questioned or doubted. The great personality was looked upon as a man who had to be taken inevitably upon his own terms. Only in the light of his own unique "personality" might one dare to justify the actions of a man. Ethical standards seemed relative when compared with those which genius deserved. This new measure for judging the human act in terms of "personality" was first applied to the extraordinary man; it soon applied for humanity at large. An ethos based upon objective goodness and truth was discarded for an ethos based in the subjective where nobility and truthfulness to one's own self prevailed.

Since personality took root in the singular, living individual, everything intended or predicated of him was expressed in terms taken from the concept of the "subject." A bearer of the only valid act, the subject became a uniting principle for all categories of activity; in turn the subject in act determined its own validity. The sharpest definition of the subject is found in the philosophy of Kant in whose system the logical, ethical, aesthetic subject is an ultimate. Beyond it nothing can be conceived. Autonomous and self-existent, the subject became the very ground for meaning in spiritual experience.

Any object derived from personality—from the subject—was looked upon as absolute; any action brought forth by personality was justified in that very act. Thus were modern man's absolutes harmonized; his absolute claim for personality wedded equably with his absolute claim for nature. From the twin standards of personality and of the natural he gained his own "morality."

Just as the mystery of inmost Nature was veiled from modern man, so was that of personality and of subjectivity. Seen as absolutes in themselves they invaded the realm of religion. The concept of personality became the basis from which "the other" was understood and judged. The man of genius, indeed, rose up as a mysterious being invested with an aura from the gods. Through this idealism in philosophy the subjectivity of the individual was united with the All, with the "world soul"; the subject was seen as its concrete expression. The personality gifted with good fortune, inner security, originality and fecundity was lauded most succinctly by Goethe. We need only be reminded of his verses from the *Westöstlichen Diwan*:

> People, serfs, and conquerors are with us always;
> But personality alone is the highest happiness
> Of the children of the earth.

It was also Goethe who gave us the most dramatic testimony for the experiences of the one in the All.

Standing between Nature and the subjective-personality was the realm of human action and of work. This realm could find its proper equilibrium only through the two poles of the subjective and the natural. Fixed therein as a third reference point for the vision of modern man was the world of history and of art. That world alone was allowed to retain an individuality proper to itself and from that world arose a third concept unique with modern man, the concept of "Culture."

The Middle Ages had wrought a world of beauty, a social order of magnificence; they had fashioned a culture of the highest reach. But everything that medieval man achieved was understood by him in the light of the service he owed to God and to God's Creation. With the Renaissance new meaning came both to the work of man and to the worker himself; meaning and value for both artist and artifact were found solely within themselves. Prior to the Renaissance only the Work of God had an absolute meaning; after the Renaissance the world ceased to be the Creation of God. It had become the work of Nature. Similarly the work of a man ceased to be an act of obedience to God's ordained service; it became a "creation" in itself. Previously a worshipper and a servant, man now took to himself the prerogatives of a "creator."

The threefold result is evident. Insofar as modern man saw the world simply as "nature," he absorbed it into himself. Insofar as he understood himself as a "personality," he made himself the Lord of his being, and insofar as he conceived a will for "culture," he strove to make of existence the creation of his own hands.

The fashioning of this three-sided vision harmonized with the conceptions upon which modern science was being built. From modern science technology has grown, and technology is a concentration of processes allowing man to posit ends in conformity with his own desires. Not only did science, politics, economics, art and pedagogy sever themselves consciously from the old bonds of Faith. Of more importance they cut themselves away from an ethic which once had bound men universally. But now each cultural discipline was to grow autonomously according to laws intrinsic to its own nature. Although modern man allowed each cultural discipline its own principles, he believed that all disciplines were interrelated through that fused Culture which grew from them separately but simultaneously supported them all. Culture was the essence of the work of man; it was independent of the Work of God. Culture arose before the vision of modern man and took its stance opposite God and His Revelation.

As with personality Culture achieved a religious significance revealing the creative mystery of the world. Within Culture the "world soul" became conscious of itself; within Culture man found the complete cause of being. Goethe expressed the full conception in his *Zalmen Xenien* when he said, "Who possesses science and art, possesses religion as well."

When faced with the question—"In how many ways can being be?"—the modern consciousness answered unhesitatingly, "The ways of being are threefold: in Nature, in subjective-personality, in Culture." The three belonged together, they conditioned and perfected one another. They created a unified framework, a finality beyond which man could not venture. That triple unity needed no verification from any other source nor did it permit the existence of any standard above itself.

[II]

I have touched but briefly upon what happened to religion after the decline of the Middle Ages when human existence was torn down and rebuilt by modern man. The issue demands careful consideration.

As taught by the Church for more than a thousand years Christian doctrine was the measure of all truth and falsity, of right and wrong. The disintegration of the Middle Ages saw the birth of a new, purely secular set of values. Dominating the growth of modern culture as it did, this new outlook was either indifferent or openly hostile toward Christianity. The defenders of Christianity complicated the problem by committing many a blunder in their battle with the new order, blunders which made Christianity seem an enemy of the human spirit.

As a result the Christian Faith was placed increasingly on the defensive. Numerous dogmatic teachings seemed to be in genuine or apparent conflict with the conclusions of philosophy and science: *e.g.*, miracles, the creation of the world and the government of God. (At the same time there arose both a new literary genre and a new spiritual attitude—the modern apologetic.) Previously Revelation and Faith had simply been the foundation, the very atmosphere of reality; now they were forced to prove their claim to truth. Even where the Faith stood most firmly it lost its placid "taken-for-granted" air; faith was strained and attenuated, even overstrained. No longer did the Faith find itself in a world belonging to it; it felt itself as a stranger in a hostile universe.

A curious religious problem emerged when the limited world picture of the Middle Ages was canceled out by the modern picture of a limitless world. To speak precisely, God lost His dwelling place; thereby man lost his proper position in existence.

In the past God's place had been on high in the Empyrean, in "heaven." Even today astronomical and religious meanings weave in and out of the word "heaven." But what terms can a man substitute, if there is no "high" place, no "beyond"? One might answer that such words imply a materialism of thought about God, Who is a Spirit and can have no "place." But such a retort is only correct in the abstract. For the concrete religious life of man God truly has His "place"—that place where the biblical "Glory to God on the Highest" has put Him. The "high place" of Heaven is both a literal and a cosmological expression of the Sovereignty of God and of the Beatitude which man is to enjoy with Him. If man's concepts allow no "high place" above or beyond the world, then the biblical Heaven has lost its definite shape. "Where" then is God?

As the contradiction of the Sublimity of God and of the blessed in heaven, the old literal and cosmological picture had seen a concrete hell, the place of hatred and abandonment. Hell itself was placed at the greatest possible distance from the Empyrean, at the bowels of the earth where classical man had also located his underworld, Hades. But if the center of the earth is "filled" with continuous matter it cannot contain the old hell. Where then is the place of damnation?

Man himself faces this same question of "place." Where is the place of man? The question seeks answer not merely as to the place man shares in nature with all corporeal things, but answer above all as to his existential place. Where is man's place in being?

The Middle Ages answered the question by insisting that man's place was the earth and the earth was the center of the universe. That answer upheld man, satisfied him in the wholeness of his responsibility, his dignity and his being. The new astronomy, however, threw the earth out of its old position; at first it lost its place as the center of the cosmos, becoming only one of the planets which circled the sun. Then, to worsen the problem, the solar system itself was absorbed within an unlimited universe. From the cosmological point of view the earth had lost all significance. Where then can man be?

We must meditate the meaning of this question carefully, for it is a question of profound importance. The Middle Ages had seen man from two points of view: he was the creature of God, a being submissive to His Will and resting in His Hand; he was also the bearer of God's Image, and belonging literally to God was destined for an eternal end. Although absolutely inferior to God, man was immeasurably greater than any other creature of the earth. Man's place in being was determined by his position in the hierarchy of living things. In every way man stood before the gaze of the Lord; on every side man governed the earth by his spiritual lordship. As the world picture changed, this position for man was also thrown into question. Man was slipping more and more into an accidental "somewhere."

In an almost inverse proportion to the medieval attempt to place man at the heart of reality, the modern consciousness has tried to tear him from the center of the world. No longer standing everywhere under the eyes of a God Whose glance enclosed the universe, man became an autonomous creature. Although removed from the very center of creation and merely a part of the world, he did have a free hand to hew his own road through life. Curiously, the new conception both exalted and debased man: he was raised up against God, exalted at His expense; he was reduced through a deep desire to an object of nature no different fundamentally from an animal or a plant. The altered picture of the world had bred both these drives in modern man.

The problem of man's place in being throws light upon the trial of Galileo. Although the negative aspects of the trial should not be excused, evidence does not prove that the trial itself resulted from spiritual obscurantism. At bottom the whole business was rooted in an anxiety about the existential foundations of being, about the place of God and of man in the economy of existence. Granted that these "places" were symbols it still holds true that a symbol is as real as a chemical or a bodily organ. Modern psychology has begun to regain a proper insight into the nature of symbolism which was self-evident to medieval man. Indeed, we may ask whether man ever recovered from the shock that racked his soul as his world turned upside down at the time of Galileo. It seems he has not recovered! Although the scientific picture of the world has become increasingly exact, man no longer finds a home within it. Insofar as man's feelings are concerned God is not at home in it.

The new world consciousness posed a number of questions for the Faith of Christian man. If the findings of the modern mind are true, how have they affected God and His Sovereignty? If God is really God, how does this truth affect the autonomous personality claimed by modern man? If he has the initiative and power promised him, how can God *really* act in the universe? If God Himself is at work governing Creation, how can man himself really act and create?

Moreover, can God really work within history if modern science and philosophy offer a true understanding of the world? Can God direct the universe providentially, can He be the Lord of Grace? Can He enter into history and become a Man? Can He establish in the world an institution which through His Authority sets itself apart from all human things; can He found a Church? Finally, if the Church has the authority she claims to possess, how can the individual be related to God as he ought to be? And if the Church is sufficient for all men, how can the individual come sincerely to God?

These and many similar problems stirred the religious life of the modern age and sought their resolution.

Most intensely modern man sought for answers within his own soul. The loss of the old, accepted vision of the world denied to man his chance of coming to terms with himself, of answering the questions posed by existence. He was shaken, insecure, exposed to the mystery of limitless realities. As occurs during all crises the depths of human nature were excited. Anguish, violence, greed, rebellion against order— more compellingly than ever these primitive drives stirred the soul of man. Both word and deed had been stripped bare by the new vision of man, shaking his deepest-held convictions. Enigmatic powers awoke out of the religious spirit; the force of the numinous impinged itself directly upon the human spirit, either from within the spirit itself or from the world at large. Not only was the numinous beneficent now but also bewildering, even destructive in its impact. Every fundamental question shook man with a new intensity: salvation and damnation, man's just relation to God, the true ordering for human life. As time passed the tensions within man's soul between the will to truth and the drive toward error, between good and evil, increased and weighed down his spirit. As the age moved on even the probity of human existence itself struck against the oppressed soul of man.

These inner tensions of spirit spread into the outer world, into history, and set in motion the great religious upheavals of the Reformation and the Counter-Reformation. Although these struggles were first linked with questions proper to theology, with the sterility of the ecclesiastical system and with the moral corruption that had invaded life at large, they also attested to the fact that the Christian life itself was to undergo a universal change.

NOTES

1. We must not overlook the fact of an operative Christian view of both the natural and the classical during the modern era and even today. This Christian affirmation has been modest, however, never forcing itself upon the corporate consciousness as the strictly modern conception has forced itself.

CHAPTER THREE

THE DISSOLUTION OF THE MODERN WORLD AND

THE WORLD WHICH IS TO COME

[I]

We have looked at the modern picture of the world in its broadest outlines. Because we are now aware of its limitations and because we know now that the modern world is coming to an end, this picture appears to us more sharply than ever before.

Until a short time ago, the three elements discussed in the preceding section of our study as intrinsic to modern life were considered an inviolable heritage. The intellectual consciousness of modern Europe as commonly delineated and accepted even in our day proclaimed those three ideals: a Nature subsisting in itself; an autonomous personality of the human subject; a culture self-created out of norms intrinsic to its own essence. The European mind believed further that the constant creation and perfection of this "culture" constituted the final goal of history. This was all a mistake. Of the many signs appearing today all point to the fact that these cherished ideals are fading from history.

My hypothesis has nothing in common, however,

with that cheap disposition which revels always in prophesying collapse or destruction. It has nothing in common with that desire which would surrender the valid achievements of modern man. Nor is my hypothesis linked with a longing for a romantically envisioned Middle Ages or with an advance into a glorified utopia of the future. But this hypothesis has its crucial importance; it will enable us both to understand and to master the meanings implicit to the new world that is upon us. That humanity was matured and deepened by its experience of the modern world cannot be denied. This truth is self-evident despite the ominous spectacle of a human nature withering beneath the destructive hand of modernity.

Our concern of the moment is neither to repudiate nor to glorify; it is to understand the modern world, to comprehend why it is coming to an end. We seek to apprehend the nature of the world epoch which is being born out of the womb of history. As yet history has not named its offspring.

[II]

If asked who expressed the modern ideal of Nature with the most classical lucidity we answer spontaneously—Goethe. We have already quoted the passage in which he phrased that ideal most powerfully. Would the man of today or, more precisely, would the man whose life and world picture lie upon this side of the first World War find his own feelings for nature expressed in this passage? I do not mean he should experience nature with the exact reverence and grandeur of a Goethe; I only ask if his emotion in the face of nature corresponds in any degree with that of a Goethe. Would the modern man relate Goethe's language from the *Tiefurtur Journal* with a heightened statement of his own less powerful, day-by-day experience of nature? I do not believe he would.

The fact that our experiences of nature, of personality and of culture deviate from those of Goethe underscores the problem we face today when we turn to Goethe's writings. The problem came to the fore this past year.[1] The Goethe of tomorrow, even to an extent the Goethe of today, cannot be the Goethe experienced by European man before the first World War. Goethe as understood formerly by modern man was understood as embodying the three ideals which buttressed the modern consciousness. That man now belongs to the past as much as they. The coming Goethe as he will be significant for the new man is not yet seen by us with any clarity.

The work of every great artist must pass through a crisis of this nature. Man first reacts toward art spontaneously; his intuitions spring from his allegiance to his common cultural and historical *milieu*. When this breaks down the old relations with a work of art disintegrate. For a time men are alienated from the work, even averse to it. The alienation and aversion will be aggravated in proportion to the vigor with which the work is defended in the name of older presuppositions and affirmations. Such denial of a work may persist until a later epoch discovers new value in it, value pertinent for man in that age. The extent to which a work of art will achieve this renaissance— through how many historic periods it can retain vigor and life—depends on the measure of human perfection incarnated in the work itself.

If I am correct, the signs of the past thirty years or more indicate that man's relations with nature are changing. Nature is no longer experienced wondrously as a rich source bestowing harmony on all things, as wisely ordered of itself, as benevolent with its favors. Man today distrusts nature, he cannot speak of "Mother Nature." Nature has become alien and dangerous to man. The religious sentiments expressed calmly and clearly by Goethe as he stood before nature are not the sentiments of man today. Nor are those expressed passionately by the Romantics or those expressed dithrambically by Hölderlin. Man has been sobered, perhaps by the disappearance of the modern sense of the infinite. Although science continues to measure distances ever more enormous in scope or more minute in detail, these measurements are always finite. And man is aware of their finiteness. The "infinity" of Giordano Bruno and of German idealism was more than a concept to express measure; it was preeminently a concept for expressing quality. It signified the godhead of the world whose being was inexhaustible, triumphant, the very origin of all things. This experience of infinity declined as the modern age drew toward its end. Today man experiences his world as finite, but a finite world cannot inspire the devotion which was inspired by the limitless cosmos of the recent past. The new sense of the finite refers not only to a limitation in expanse but also to a limitation in the core of being, at the heart of matter. Since the world is finite, it is fragile; since the cosmos is expanding, its very being is a venture. It is menaced and endangered on every side and becomes the more glorious and precious. Man now feels responsible for his universe; man must now take care of being. We feel that man has taken the universe into his own heart; we know that this act spells mystery. It seems as though some powerless force in being were groping for the hand of man. It seems as though some drama as yet undefinable were being prepared at the heart of the world, a drama which needs the heart of man.

The religious movements of our time pose so many contradictions that one can scarcely find a coherent trend common to them all. To reach for the intangibles which may underlie them, we must seek answers for any number of questions. What caused the religious emotion of Rilke and how is it related to the venture into being of existentialist philosophy? What depths of the human spirit, what inner currents of the soul, are being uncovered by the newly serious study of myths today? How should we view the grim magnificence, the possibilities and dangers, promised by modern scientific-physical theory? How must we evaluate the titanism which inspires politics and technics now? These are but a few of the questions which must be given unifying answers before we can bring coherence to the religious attitudes of the new man.

Assuredly the world as a whole no longer encompasses and shelters man as once it did; it has become a far different thing. And it has gained thereby new significances for the religious life of man.

The world outlook now being born or, more precisely, the tendencies within that outlook refuse to venerate nature; that is, they deny to nature the kind of veneration experienced by Goethe himself. And we must recall that Goethe had made that relation central to man's experience of nature. This shifting relationship manifests itself even as it leaves itself undefined in the striking complex of knowledge, theory, skill and mode of production summed up in the term "technics," that is in technology. During the nineteenth century technology developed slowly; for that stretch of time it developed only at the hands of a non-technologized mentality. Then at last in the decades just prior to the second World War and the years of that War, the man motivated by technology broke into the field of history and took possession. This technological man experiences nature neither as a standard of value nor as a living shelter for his spirit.

The technological mind sees nature as an insensate order, as a cold body of facts, as a mere "given," as an object of utility, as raw material to be hammered into useful shape; it views the cosmos similarly as a mere "space" into which objects can be thrown with complete indifference. Technological man will remold the world; he sees his task as Promethean and its stakes as being and non-being.

The modern era was fond of justifying technology and rested its defense upon the argument that technology promoted the well-being of man. In doing so it masked the destructive effects of a ruthless system. I do not believe that the age to come will rest with such an argument. The man engaged today in the labor of "technics" knows full well that technology moves forward in final analysis neither for profit nor for the well-being of the race. He knows in the most radical sense of the term that power is its motive—a lordship of all; that man seizes hold of the naked elements of both nature and human nature. His action bespeaks immense possibilities not only for "creation" but also for destruction, especially for the destruction of humanity itself. Man as a human being is far less rooted and fixed within his own essence than is commonly accepted. And the terrible dangers grow day by day. Once the "autonomous" state has broken all bonds, it will be able to deliver the last *coup de grâce* to human nature itself. Man's relations with nature have reached the point of final crisis: man will either succeed in converting his mastery into good—then his accomplishment would be immense indeed—man will either do that or man himself will be at an end.

Within this area of choice an emotion partaking of the religious seems to penetrate again. This religious feeling has no link with the natural piety of Giordano Bruno or of Goethe; rather, it is bound up intrinsically with the dangers for himself and for his earth which man has found locked up with his technological power.

The new religious emotion wells up from a sense of the profound loneliness which man knows in the midst of all that is now summed up by the term "the World"; man's emotion grows out of the realization that he approaches his ultimate decision, that he must face it with responsibility, with resolution and with bravery.

[III]

Man's attitude towards personality and subjectivity are undergoing a change analogous to that found with nature.

We recall that man's former view of personality developed from the reactions which he experienced when he was torn from the ties of the Middle Ages, when he became lord of his being, when he took upon himself the prerogatives of autonomy. The new attitude was expressed severally: in philosophy by the theory of the subject as the ground of all concepts; in politics by the notion of bourgeois freedom; and in ethics by the assumption that the individual man bore within himself his own form. That form both enabled and obliged him to develop according to its resources; it was destined to bring into being a unique individuality.

These new points of view were connected with a definite sociological type, the "middle class." Taken in its broadest sense, the term "middle class" included not only those men who sought a rational clarity of thought while they yearned for security but also those men who

were their antithesis, the romantics and the bohemians.
The middle class included in its ranks exceptional men
and common men, men of genius and mediocrities.
The rise of technology is creating a radically different
sociological type and attitude. The new man finds the
ideal of the self-made and creative personality inimical;
he refuses to grant that the autonomous subject is the
measure of human perfection.

Sharpest evidence for the denial of the older idea
of personality comes with that human type—who
stands at the extreme pole from the autonomous—the
Mass Man. When used in this connection the term
does not connote a man who is worthless; it simply
designates the man who is absorbed by technology
and rational abstraction. This new human type strikes
us unfavorably at first because it has entered history
with no tradition of its own; in fact, it must assert itself
against those traditions which until now have held the
day. Mass man carries within his nature the seeds of an
historic growth proper to his situation just as did the
men who went before him. He will not, however, find
solutions for the problem of existence; he will not succeed in turning the earth into a paradise. The men
who went before him could not do these things nor
can he. But mass man does bear the future within him;
he bears that tomorrow which will last until the day
after tomorrow.

The vast majority of the men of the past existed
in formless crowds. They differed sharply in their
development from those individuals who had succeeded in achieving for themselves that perfection

which developed to the hilt their inherent possibilities. As the extraordinary individual became the standard of human excellence the mediocre multitude acted as a backdrop, as the source for those accomplishments required by day-to-day living. Ordinary persons also strove to become individuals in their own right; they aspired for their own distinct style of life. Within the contemporary scene, however, the masses present an altogether different social reality. The mass is not a multitude of men undeveloped but perfectible; from the first it possessed a distinctly organized social structure throughout itself. The mass was fashioned according to the law of standardization, a law dictated by the functional nature of the machine. Moreover, the most highly developed individuals of the mass, its elite, are not merely conscious of the influence of the machine; they deliberately imitate it, building its standards and rhythms into their own ethos. As a social phenomenon it must be repeated, however, the mass is not debased and decayed essentially as was the rabble of ancient Rome. The mass has assumed a genuine form of existence in human history; it is original and capable of both cultural expansion and fuller realization of its own potentialities. We make this evaluation, of course, only in the light of those standards which are intrinsic to mass man himself; we cannot base it upon the standards which belonged to modern man.

For example, we cannot link personality and subjectivity with mass man under the definitions of those terms given earlier in this essay. Mass man has no desire for independence or originality in either the management or the conduct of his life. Nor does he seek to create an environment belonging only to himself, reflecting only his self. The gadgets and technics forced upon him by the patterns of machine production and of abstract planning mass man accepts quite simply; they are the forms of life itself. To either a greater or a lesser degree mass man is convinced that his conformity is both reasonable and just. Similarly, the new man of the masses has no desire to live his life according to principles which are uniquely his own. Neither liberty of external action nor freedom of internal judgment seem for him to have unique value. And understandably so, for he has never experienced them. As a simple matter of course mass man unites himself with any "organization" modeled after the mass itself; there he obeys whatever program is placed before him. In this fashion "The Man Without Personality" finds himself placed on the one road which will assuredly carry him through life. Of even more significance the regimented instincts of this new human type forbid him to appear distinctive, compel him to appear anonymous. Mass man acts almost as if he felt that to be one's self was both the source of all injustice and even a sign of peril.

One might object that personality is exhibited by the leaders in mass society who help in fashioning this new type of man. One might claim that these leaders reflect a new kind of mastery, a new form of human greatness. But, it must be reiterated, this is not the case. The new leader is co-ordinated by the very masses he leads; he does not possess a creative personality in the old sense; he is not that former individual who always flowered under exceptional circumstances. The leader is nothing but the complement of the many. Although performing different and higher functions, he is but another in essence with the many.

With the loss of personality comes the steady fading away of that sense of uniqueness with which man had once viewed his own existence, which had once been the source of all social intercourse. It is taken increasingly for granted that man ought to be treated as an object. Man confronts this attitude in the range of authority exercised over him; he may merely meet it in countless statistics and tables or he may experience its culmination in an unspeakable rape of the individual, of the group, even of the whole nation. And these actions have occurred. Not only have they occurred under the pressing crisis and misery of war but also during the normal function and administration of government.

It may seem that we treat these phenomena unjustly, since we have described mass man exclusively in terms of his lack of veneration for nature, of his denial of personality and of his moral insensitivity in using force. These ethical deficiencies are certainly found in mass man, but they do not offer in themselves a full understanding either of their widespread practice or of their stoic acceptance by their victims.

The whole process has been furthered and supported by an integral change in the way that man experiences both himself and his fellow men.

This change can have one of two consequences. The individual will either disappear into the collective mass as an empty means for a mechanical function—this is the terrible danger which lies brooding over history today—or he will appear to accept the standardized pattern of social life, adjusting to his loss of liberty both for free decision and for open growth as a person. Indeed that liberty is no longer his even to renounce. If he takes the latter course, he will do so for the sake of consolidating his own inner life, of conserving—at least for a time—the core of his spiritual existence.

The fact that the term "personality" is disappearing from daily use and is being replaced by the term "person" is not without meaning. In the first place the term has a strong stoic flavor. Looking toward definition rather than toward growth, it does not suggest the rich and extraordinary but the frugal and limited. Yet these attributes of the human deserve also to be nurtured and guarded. Here we touch upon the second meaning which the term "person" bears. It helps to define the incommunicable being possessed by man, an inviolability which depends neither on special talents nor on social station. It simply emerges from the fact that a man has been called forth by God. To assert and cherish the incommunicability of each and every man is not to advance self-interest or privilege; it is to pledge that loyalty, that fundamental duty, which is one with being a man.

We must not talk about the mass, however, without seeking its positive significance. It is clear that the values of the past cannot be recaptured as long as history is dominated by the collective mass rather than by richly developed individuals. Indeed it is difficult to discover any new possibilities for humanity in a future relinquished to the mass. At the same time, the man seeking to probe this issue must be certain that he does not root his investigation in spontaneous emotions or involuntary reactions which find inspiration in values belonging only to the past. He must make a decisive effort to overcome his own prejudices, to expose himself freely to an order which may menace his very essence, stamped as it is with the forces of history.

First, then, what irrevocably is a man? A man is a person called by God. As that man he is capable of answering for his own actions and of participating in reality through an inner and innate source which is one with himself. This capacity makes each man unique. A man is not unique because of his peculiar talents; a man is unique in the clear and absolute sense that, as is each of his fellows, he is a being one with himself, indispensable, irreplaceable, inviolate. Because the unique is so, as man it is good that it be multiplied. It is good that many men exist, that each one of them be offered the chance for personal growth. The objection to this affirmation is obvious, however, in that clear sense in which one may say that a hundred men are less important than one man or that the greatest values come always from the very few. Yet such a rejoinder runs the risk of slipping away from the stark value of the personal into a realm of accidents—originality, accomplishment, cultural worth.

The text, "What does it profit a man if he gain the whole world and suffer the loss of his soul?" bears application here. The "winning of the world" encompasses all those things which exist within the area of social-cultural values: fullness of life, richness of personality, "Art and Science," each in its many forms. Yet involved with all these ends we find the human soul in its loss or its sanctification—man at the crossroads confronting the Call of God. Faced by the decision "the world" vanishes.

Have we a right, then, to advance any final judgment of mass man because his increasing dominance hems in cultural and personality values? Because the cultural level of a thousand men must necessarily be lower than that of ten, have we a right to maintain that only the ten should be born but not the thousand? Is not the very right to personal being an unconditional right which ranks above all other considerations? This poses an urgent question for the individualist today. In an absolute sense, to what height is he willing to advance the social-cultural goals he defends, goals which of themselves he is perfectly entitled to defend?

Instead of protesting against the rising masses in the name of a culture built upon personality values, would it not be wiser to seek out the human problems of the mass itself? They lie within this double question: does the leveling which flows from the dominance of the many cause the loss of personality or does it cause the loss of the person himself? The first consequence may occur; the second, never.

Even when the question—are the masses free to develop personality?—is asked with urgency and force, it cannot be answered by the standards of the old personality culture. It must be answered by conditions proper to the mass itself. Moving away from the assumptions proper to the rich fullness, to the freedom of the old personality culture, we have found that man becomes genuinely a "Person" when he is faced toward God, is left inviolate in his dignity, is robed with duties no other can assume. We feel justified in assuming at this time that the genuine "Person" is destined to stand forth with a spiritual resoluteness never demanded of man before. Strangely, the very mass which carries the danger of utilitarianism and totalitarianism also offers the fullest range of spiritual maturity to the human person. Such a challenge demands an inner freedom and strength of character, a strengthening of character which we can scarcely conceive. Nothing else, however, can withstand the powers of anonymity which grow more immense day by day.

At this point another consideration arises. If we do not read the history of the past hundred years as a process of decay, then what positive meaning does it have? It is found without doubt in the value achieved by man as he shoulders the work of dominating his world. That work will make such tremendous demands of man that he could never achieve it by individual initiative or even by the united effort of men bred to an individualistic way.

The work of dominating the world calls for a union of skills and a unity of achievement that can only grow from quite a different attitude. This new attitude is revealed by the evident fact that the coming man renounces an idiosyncratic life for a communal form, that he surrenders individual initiative for a given order of things. The process of conformity has profaned so many areas of life and has done so much violence to man that we are apt to neglect its positive meaning, a meaning which it does possess. It lies behind the immensity of the work to be done; it lies in the corresponding greatness of man's position as he faces his task, in his sense of solidarity with it, in his comradeship for his fellow workers. When all other substantial values have disintegrated comradeship remains. This fact can and ought to be understood, I think, as a sign of what is to come. The new comradeship will be a comradeship in the task of preserving being itself, a comradeship in the work of facing future danger and menace. If this comradeship is accepted in accord with the true meaning of "Person," it will be the supreme human value to come from the mass. Even under the changing conditions brought by the mass, comradeship could help to regain the values of the "Person": benevolence, understanding and justice.

These considerations force us to conclude that democratic values as much as they are reiterated demand careful and sober reflection. The crisis which confronts democracy has arisen because it received its historical imprint from the attitudes of a personality culture. Thus democratic values presumed a small population. It is evident that a genuine democratic spirit, in that sense, is only possible in small countries or in the large country which possesses great spaces of open land. The effectiveness of democratic values for the new age is problematical. Can they be reintegrated by the person facing the meagre and stark conditions of human life as it will be lived in the future? Can they revitalize him in his life within the mass?

Without those values another and terrible possibility could emerge; man might succumb to the power of the anonymous. And we must not lose sight of yet another issue. Well into the modern age, the ideals of human existence were supported by the conception of a "human man." The term does not involve a moral judgment; rather it describes a kind of man who can do either good or evil. This "human man" appeared in many guises during the course of history: as the man of antiquity, as the man of the Middle Ages, as the modern man until the turn of the century. His portraits differ sharply from one another, yet they have one thing in common: each delineates the kind of man whom we have defined as the "human man" capable of good or evil.

Perhaps we can add that the crucial factor in the development of the "human man" was that his field of activities coincided with his field of experience. The realities he knew basically were the things of nature as his senses enabled him to see, to hear and to touch them. The things which he made were brought forth essentially by the labor of his body, even when it was extended and strengthened by those auxiliaries we call tools. The cumulative effect of tool power was often extremely great; indeed the principles of the machine were already known to antiquity and the Middle Ages, while from its very inception the modern age developed machinery scientifically and technologically. Although the modern world deeply felt the impact of scientific and technical development, it did not become radically different from that impact. The basic structure and culture of the modern world was not changed. Scientific development remained within the range of those things which man could grasp with his senses, picture with his imagination or experience with his emotions. Thus the ambitions and achievements of modern man were harmonized with his dual nature, with his body and with his soul. Similarly with modern man when he confronted nature; he used the energies he found in nature; he utilized its materials; he developed its forms. Man ruled nature by fitting himself into it, but he left the status of nature in existence fundamentally inviolate.

From the standpoint of man's relations with nature, the term "human" signified a set of genuine experiences. Just as he had established an elastic, harmonious proportion between himself and nature, so he used the possibilities and ends which he discovered in nature from his immediate sensations. In all man was "human" because he both experienced and lived through the very works which he bred and produced from the union of nature and his own self.

These relations between man and nature changed. Growth in knowledge, ambition and human aspiration increasingly shouldered aside the older "human" value; first in isolated instances, then more frequently, finally as a simple matter of course. The old order uniting man's immediate life and his culture was completely swept aside. Man today knows far more intellectually and scientifically than he can even represent to himself: *e.g.*, the vast universes of new solar systems known by astronomy. Man can plan and execute projects now which, quite simply, he cannot experience at all: *e.g.*, the technical projects made possible by modern physics.

Man's relations with nature have been altered radically, have become indirect. The old immediateness has been lost, for now his relations are transmitted by mathematics or by instruments. Abstract and formalized, nature has lost all concreteness; having become inorganic and technical, it has lost the quality of real experience.

As a result man's experience of his own work has changed. It too has become distant, indirect, abstract, dead. Man can no longer experience the work he does; he can only calculate its possibilities and control its effects from a distance. This condition raises graver problems. Basically man becomes himself, is himself through what he experiences. What can he *be*, however, if he can no longer involve himself "sensibly" in the work he does? Human responsibility means simply that man must give an account of what he does. Responsibility involves growth, growth from an immature process of executing material acts to a mature process of squaring them with ethical standards. But how can ethical standards be applied to areas of work which have become lost in abstract formulae and distant machines?

The man leading such a work-life we call the "non-human."[2] Again this term is not used to express a moral judgment any more than was the term "human man." It signifies a man shaped by a certain cultural pattern, an historic pattern which the passage of time increasingly sharpens. He is a man of increasing alienations between his experience and his understanding, between his experience and his field of work.

Under the impact of this historic change, we must repeat, man's relations with nature have changed radically. Man himself is less capable of attaining nature, of representing it and of experiencing it.

Giordano Bruno, Montaigne, Rousseau and Spinoza, Goethe and Hölderlin, even the materialists to the very end of the nineteenth century, understood "Nature" as that totality of things and events which man encountered around and about him. "Nature" acted as a springboard from which he projected his experiences in an ever-widening circle. It was that mould of forms, that realm of processes given to man through immediate sensations with which he stood in harmony. The forms and processes of nature were *there*, before man, accessible to his understanding and sensibility, capable of being directly experienced. Everything has begun to retreat today into inaccessibility. It is quite true, of course, that in the earlier sense nature was "mysterious" even in the open light of day, but this mystery was congenial to man. He could still address nature as "Mother Nature"; therein man could find a home; he experienced birth and growth, suffering and death through nature as well. But today man can no longer approach nature directly; it has become ominous and distant.

Lacking concreteness any more nature can only be conceptualized abstractly, and it becomes more and more an intricate network of relations and functions which can only be grasped by mathematical formulae, which is supported by "something" no longer permitting direct expression.

The new nature of mass man is beyond our common experience. If experienced by a few here and there, it is done in an enigmatic way through an order of things to which man cannot speak. Yet perhaps we should exercise more caution in this evaluation. There may be possibilities for fresh experience within the new nature. The tasks facing man might imply that the boundaries of his experience can be extended, that an immense universe of reality formerly unexperienced in its effects was now being opened to man. The work confronting man might also imply that a kind of indirect experience was coming into the world, whereby that which had been only abstract thought was now being absorbed into the living experience of man.[3]

Undoubtedly man must be on his guard against this new nature; as well, he must shoulder a stern sense of responsibility for it. This responsibility is linked with the problems of personality discussed above, problems to which we shall return.

This nature (we keep the term "nature" because man has kept it and we want to be understood) is no longer a "natural nature," in the sense that the "natural" implied something immediately perceived and immediately reacted to by man. The new nature is not self-evident to perception or to understanding; rather it is a "not-natural Nature." Once again the term is descriptive not moral.

It is clear, of course, that the flower on the table remains the blooming and fragrant beauty it has always been; the garden outside is forever a source of perennial freshness brought close to the hand of man. Mountain and sea and the star-studded sky appear to the man contemplating them with the same vastness as of old, liberating and immense in sweep. But even here the effects of technology must be considered, of "technology" in its most universal application: seen in relation to irrigation and transportation, to the tourist and amusement industries, seen in relation to everything which destroys nature in its primitive originality.

At the same time, sincere attempts are being made in many areas of life—*e.g.*, in mental health and in the rearing and education of children—to restore to nature all that is proper to it. These efforts retain their complete significance and value today. Man has the right, a right in self-defense, to seek the original freshness of his dual nature—in his body and in his soul—in order to feel at home again even in this lost world of symbols which has been advanced within the last decades, which has been demanded by all the exertions of technological man.

Every man who meditates on these issues senses the need for decision which confronts him. If his decision is essentially romantic, it calls for a return to a relationship with a nature which no longer exists. If his decision is realistic, it points toward an integration with the coming world, an integration through which the "natural" is saved. (In the past this saving was attempted through fruitless, irrelevant "life" reforms.) Not only must the "natural" be defended against the new world, however, but also it must be regained by forwarding its growth from within that world itself. These tasks are closely related to those confronting man in his work to keep personality from dying.

These two phenomena, the not-human man and the not-natural nature, promise to be the foundations upon which the world of the future will be erected. Man will then face an existence in which he will be free to further his lordship of creation, carrying it even to its last consequences. This mastery will be open to him because he has permitted himself utter freedom: the freedom to determine his own goals, to dissolve the immediate reality of things, to employ its elements for the execution of his own ends. These things he will do without any consideration for what had been thought inviolate or untouchable in nature. He will ignore that strong sense of the sacredness of nature which had endured within mankind's earlier vision of the world.

[IV]

Because we find ourselves at the center of these changing processes, it has been far from easy to describe the changes which occurred in the relations between modern man and subjectivity, between modern man and nature. Yet it is even more difficult to express what is happening to the concept of culture. Here too there is change, but the change consists not merely in the search for new objects or methods for effecting an ever more complete cultural order; rather it seems to consist chiefly in an alteration of the entire concept of "culture."

Men today find it difficult to comprehend the significance which cultural activities had during the earlier phases of modern life. Then culture surged at full tide; it was the springtime of its being; it possessed an extravagant, inexhaustible fullness, an uncontrollable optimism for the future. Mathematics and the natural sciences developed with rapid stride. The pages of antiquity were opened as history began its inexhaustible work. Man's fascination with man himself was awakened as he observed the multiform activities of man. The new sciences of anthropology and psychology analyzed and studied man's ways; political science observed human society as a great living organism, examined its growth, its many rich flowerings, its conditions of existence. Philosophy freed itself from the bonds of theology and became man's direct investigation into the phenomena of his world; art in each of its forms—sculpture, plastic art, poetry, drama—became an autonomous activity producing a wealth of artistic genres. The national states matured, each forming itself upon a conscious awareness of its own tremendous power. Boldly, excitedly, modern man took possession of the entire globe. As the seas and the continents were explored colonies were established. By means of all those inventions and procedures—inconceivable to an earlier age—which we call technics man came to dominate nature. Finally, technics were joined indissolubly with an economy of uncontrolled greed. Thus was begotten the many-faceted system of modern capitalism. These consequences were like an eruption; from the depths had sprung unknown powers hitherto sealed off from the sight of man. Man was able to experience the whole world; through that experience he experienced himself as an entirely new being. He was inspired by excessive confidence; now a marvelous and genuine future would begin to flower. Everything of the past had been but obstacle or preparation.

Modern man had convinced himself that he stood at last before reality as it was. The springs of existence would be opened before him. The energies of a nature now accessible to his understanding would blend with those of his own nature and the "great life"

would be realized. Knowledge, commerce, production, each would perfect itself according to its own
laws. All the spheres of reality would be united into an
overwhelming harmony. Yet that achieved whole—
"culture" itself—would continue to expand and within
it man would fulfill himself.

Modern faith in progress was the doctrine which
manifested these aspirations, and man's faith in
progress grew confidently, based in a logic of human
nature and its accomplishments. The laws of nature,
the psychological and real structure of human life, the
relationships among individuals and the forms by
which the social whole conducted itself, each was
united with the other by an inner necessity—bred by
and breeding "culture." Their union would stimulate
still further growth toward what was "better."

We do not hold this doctrine any more. On the contrary, we recognize with increasingly clarity that the
modern world deceived itself.

This doubt does not mean that we want to criticize
the cultural achievements of the modern age. That has
been done already by others—from the trusting peda-
gogue to the pessimistic skeptic. Their criticisms began
at the very moment of history when modern achievements mounted most triumphantly. At the zenith of
European growth—rising from the Renaissance and
Baroque periods—Rousseau had said that culture was
only good within a narrow framework; beyond that
framework it was largely something evil. He cautioned
men to return to nature, which alone was true and guiltless. Attitudes such as Rousseau's merely point to the

fact, after all, that progress should be kept moderate and controlled. They do not question progress itself. Only the Christian critique has that deeper penetration. From Revelation itself, the Christian critique knows that man stands in danger of losing himself in the world and in his work. The judgment of Christianity knows "one necessity." Because of this it was able to see through the optimisms of progress: first, its enthusiasms; later, its elevated status as a dogma. The Christian judgment knows the falsehood of autonomous areas of human activity. It knows that a cultural order which does away with God cannot prevail—simply because God exists. These doubts and criticisms come from Revelation; they rise up from beyond the walls of modern culture. Although they are just, they have remained historically ineffective.

By contrast, the doubts and criticisms of culture today come from within culture itself, for we no longer trust it. We cannot accept culture as it was accepted during the modern age, as a meaningful realm of life or as a dependable rule for action. Culture has lost all kinship with the "objective spirit," with that crucible which contains the truth of existence itself. We feel that the "culture" of modern man lacked harmony; we must guard against culture for several reasons: it has been repudiated historically; it is marked by defects; most crucially it is engraved with basic intentions and standards of value which are simply false. No one today can trust the work of man as the modern world trusted it. No one today can trust the work of man any more than he can trust nature.

In offering this critique, however, we must certainly

admit the sources of our own failures. Such a critique might be identified with the pessimism of a nation which was conscious—in an absolute sense—of its own decadence. It might be associated with the black spirit in the West which feels that it has aged, that leadership has passed to younger nations. Be that as it may, the Christian premises of the critique are valid.

The modern mind took culture to be a "natural" thing. We know, of course, that culture is not natural in any real sense; indeed, true culture rests upon the ability of the human spirit both to distinguish itself from and to stand opposite to the natural order of things surrounding it. For the modern consciousness, however, nature and spirit were formed into a unified whole, a whole which constituted the totality of being, creation itself, and in which everything was necessary and everything perfect. These convictions formed the very foundation of modern man's optimism about culture.

History has proved his convictions erroneous. The human spirit is free to do evil as well as good, to destroy as well as to build. The power of destruction is not intrinsic to the structure of reality as its negative mode necessarily; rather it is a power of negation in the most primitive sense of the latter term. Evil is done, but there is no reason why it had to be done; it would have been possible to do good, but the good was not done. The facts prove that man often takes an evil road. Our age is aware of the reality of the deliberate destructiveness in the human spirit and our age is troubled to its very depths. Therein lies its greatest opportunity: to grasp the truth by breaking away from the optimisms of the modern mind.

This chance to break away from the illusions of the modern mind reveals itself in many areas of contemporary culture—in science, philosophy, sociology, education and literature. Each of these disciplines has seen man under a false light, false in the reading of details and false fundamentally; therefore false in final judgment of the human condition.

Man is not the reality that either positivism or materialism made him out to be. In these philosophies, man "evolved" out of an animal life which had itself proceeded from a previous differentiation of matter. In spite of the many traits that man has in common with other living beings, however, man is a being distinct from them all. He is stamped with that which is essentially his own—his spirit—and the spirit could not have come from any material source. Man's possession of spirituality determines everything that he is and that he had, radically. Man is endowed, therefore, with a nature which at root is not that of any other living thing.

Nor is man the creature that idealism makes of him. Although idealism espouses the spiritual, it equates the human with the absolute spirit while applying to absolute spirit the principles of evolution. In idealism, the absolute spirit developed by a process which is equated with the evolution of the world itself. Man is simply absorbed within this sweeping activity. Consequently, he possesses no freedom in any forthright sense nor does he truly carve his destiny by an initiative proper to himself. Man is not this creature of the idealist, however. Man may be finite, but he is also a real person—irreplaceable in his unique act of being—one whose dignity cannot be supplanted, whose responsibility cannot be avoided. Moreover, history does not move along its course directed from without by the logic of an absolute spirit which is the very being of the world; it moves forward only as determined by the freedom of man.

And finally, man is not as existentialism makes him out to be. For the existentialist man is man minus any presuppositions—either essential or ethical. Man is simply free. He must determine himself not only in his actions but also in his very being. Thrown into a chaos and without a place therein, man has only himself, and beyond all he is condemned to create his own fate. This bleakness is not true. Man possesses an essential self which empowers him to say, "I am this or I am that." An order of reality exists which empowers man to say, "I am at this moment standing here in a certain place among all the things that are." A world of sensation does exist, a world which surrounds man in its totality; it may threaten him, but it also supports him.

No man truly aware of his own human nature will admit that he can discover himself in the theories of modern anthropology—be they biological, psychological, sociological or any other. Only the accidents of man—his attributes, his relations, his forms—make up these theories; they never take man simply as he is. They speak about man, but they never really see man. They approach him, but they never truly find him.

They handle him, but they never grip him as he actually is. They take hold of him by statistics; they integrate him into organizations; they put him into use. Forever they play out the same grotesque and fearful comedy, but its incidents strike always upon a phantom. Even when man is subjected to forces which misuse him or mutilate or destroy him, he is not the creature at all which those forces aim to subject.

As seen by the contemporary mind man does not exist. The mind of today attempts continually to lock man into categories where he will not fit. Mechanical, biological, psychological or sociological abstractions are all variations of a basic urge to make man one with "nature," even if it be a "nature of the spirit." But a vital reality escapes this type of mind; namely, man's very act of being which constitutes a man in the primitive, absolute sense, which makes man a man at the very core of his self, which makes him a finite person existing. This is what the existing man is even when he does not want to be, even when he denies his own nature. Called by God into being, man encounters other things and persons in existence, but the new mind does not see that in those relations man is a person possessed of a marvelous yet frightful freedom, that he is capable of conserving or of destroying the world, that he is capable of fulfilling or of surrendering and destroying himself in his very substance. The new mind has not seen that the power for destruction does not proceed from outside or above the human person; it has not seen that the power of evil is the truly negative, which can be avoided and which at root is utterly senseless.

The same absence of vision is manifested—more sharply, more urgently—in the dangers which daily arise from culture itself. And these dangers menace culture even as they menace the men who bear within themselves the cultural order.

This added danger comes from many and varied sources; especially does it come from that power over existence which is the very foundation for present cultural growth. Modern man believed that an increase of power meant an increase of "progress" itself, that it advanced man in his security, usefulness, welfare and vigor; it was an assimilation of new values into the stream of culture. Power, however, is truly a thing more powerful than any of those things. It can create evil as well as good; it can destroy as well as construct. What happens to power depends upon man's tempered exercise of it, upon the reasoned ends to which he places it. Close examination proves that recent years have been marked by a monstrous growth in man's power over being, over things and over men, but the grave responsibility, the clear consciousness, the strong character needed for exercising this power well have not kept pace with its growth at all. Contemporary man has not been trained to use power well nor has he—even in its loosest sense—an awareness of the problem itself. He seems alert to the crisis of power today only in its limited external dangers, such as clearly arose during the recent War and were then publicly discussed.

These observations imply that the risk is growing day by day that man will not use his power as he should. The present lack of an ethic—one both true and effective—for controlling power's use tends to breed further illusion. The use of power is accepted simply as another natural process; its only norms are taken from alleged necessity, from either utility or security. Power is never considered in terms of the responsibility for choice which is inherent in freedom.

Of even more significance, the development of power has created the impression that power objectifies itself; that is, power cannot really be possessed or even used by man; rather, it unfolds independently from the continuous logic of scientific investigations, from technical problems, from political tensions. The conviction grows that power simply demands its own actualization.

Yes, this does mean that power has become demonic. The term "demonic" is torn and tattered of true reference, as are all the important words bearing on human existence. Therefore, we must bring careful reflection to its real meaning before we apply it further.

There is no being without a master. As far as being is nature—or the non-personal creation—being belongs to God, Whose will is expressed in the laws by which this being, this nature, exists. As far as being is taken out of nature and into the sphere of human freedom, it belongs to man and man is responsible for it. If man fails in his responsibility and does not care for being as he should, it does not return to nature. To think that it does is a negligent assumption, one with which the contemporary world has consoled itself with more or less awareness. But being is not something which one can dispose of by putting it away in storage. When man fails in his responsibility toward the being which he has taken from nature, that being becomes the possession of something anonymous.

We may express this psychologically by saying that being is then governed by the unconscious. The unconscious, however, is a chaotic disorder in which the possibilities for destruction are at least as strong as those for healing or consolation. Nor does this end the story. Demons may take possession of the faculties of man if he does not answer for them with his conscience. We do not use the word "demons" as it is used in an ephemeral journalism. We are using the term in the precise sense given it by Revelation. We mean spiritual beings who were created whole and good by God, but who fell away from Him by electing for evil and who are bent on befouling His Creation. These are the demons, then, who rule man once he has abdicated his responsibilities. They rule him through his apparently natural but really contradictory instincts, through his apparently logical but in truth easily influenced reason. They rule him through the brutality committed by his helpless selfishness. If we reflect upon the events of the last years without either rationalistic or naturalistic prejudices, man's manner of conduct, his intellectual and psychological vagaries, speak to us with sufficient clarity of these things.

The modern world forgot the fact of "demons"

because it had blinded itself by its revolutionary faith in autonomy. The modern world thought that man could simply have power and rest secure in its exercise. Some kind of logic inherent in things forced them to behave in the realm of human freedom as dependably as they behaved in the realm of nature. This assumption is false. The moment that energy or matter or a natural form is grasped by man, it receives a new character. No longer is it simply a part of nature; it has become part of the world surrounding man, which world is man's own "creation." The thing of nature becomes involved with, even partakes of, human freedom; in so doing it also partakes of human frailty. It has become ambivalent, carrying a potential for evil as well as good.

When a chemical is found in a living organism, it has properties other than it has in pure form or as a mineral. It has become a part of that organism, for it has been absorbed into its very structure and function. To say that oxygen is oxygen—except as an abstraction—is not only unscientific but also naive. The concrete determination of oxygen belongs strictly with its existential relationships. Similarly, an organ in the body of an animal is far different from the same organ in the body of a man. In a man it enters into the living form of the spirit, into its affections, its rational and ethical experiences; thus it wins new possibilities for achievement and for destruction. We do not expect "the heart" of an animal to be like the heart of a man; to do so would indeed be a primitive materialism.

Yet such a primitive attitude was apparent in that

modern optimism which thought that "culture" was intrinsically secure. A true culture, on the other hand, bespeaks the admission of "being" from nature into the realm of human freedom where it takes on the potentialities of that new order of being. Natural "being" is thus transformed, in a sense, and given new areas for activity. It is endangered, however, and can bring ruin and disaster, if it is not elevated by man, as it demands, into the order of the personal and the moral. Could the events of the last decades have happened at the peak of a really true culture in Europe? This frightful destruction did not drop down from heaven; in truth it rose up out of hell! A culture marked by a true ordering could not have invented such incomprehensible systems of degradation and destruction. Monstrosities of such conscious design do not emerge from the calculations of a few degenerate men or of small groups of men; they come from processes of agitation and poisoning which had been long at work. What we call moral standards—responsibility, honor, sensitivity of conscience—do not vanish from humanity at large if men have not already been long debilitated. These degradations could never have happened if its culture had been as supreme as the modern world thought.

But it must still be reiterated; the modern age acted as if the substance of creation would remain as secure as it was in the natural order after it had been brought into the sphere of human freedom. The modern mind presumed that that second degree of nature—if a trifle more complicated, if a shade less stable—could be depended upon as it could be in the order of nature itself. This facile conclusion bred a carelessness, even an irresponsibility, in the management of existence which becomes incomprehensible upon reflection, upon closer examination of the history of cultural realities. From this irresponsibility an ever-increasing danger arose, a danger both material and spiritual, threatening the works of man, the life of man and of humanity.

The awareness of what happened to modern man and his world is growing, but whether it is growing rapidly enough to stem the diseases which threaten to engulf the entire earth—diseases exceeding the disaster of war—is a moot question. In any event the bourgeois superstition of relying upon "progress" has been shattered. Many men now suspect that "culture" is not at all what the modern age thought it to be; many suspect that culture is not a realm of beautiful security but a game of dice. Its stakes are life and death, but nobody knows how the last die will be cast.

We have spoken of a "non-human man" and of a "non-natural nature." We must now find a term to express the character which will belong to the culture of the future. I confess frankly that I have been unable to find one. The two former terms are so apt to mislead of themselves. The term "human," for example, includes the concept "man," so that my term literally reads the "un-human." At the same time, the fact remains that we are concerned with man. We are forced to conclude, it seems, that the question demands a complete, a radical penetration into the meaning of "man" himself; it demands a final judgment which will determine the ultimate essence of man. This judgment cannot proceed from "nature"; it must issue from man's essence itself. Similarly, the chosen term "non-natural nature" seems to neutralize itself, since "nature" has designated whatever science discovered concerning the essences of things themselves.

I can only hope, therefore, that the reader will take both terms in the *historic* sense in which they are intended. The term "human" points to that particular form of human nature which served as the criterion for human excellence from classical antiquity until the most recent years. The term "natural" pointed to that picture of the external world which that kind of man saw around and about him and to which he related himself.

I know of no term with which to designate the culture of the future; to speak of a "non-cultural culture" would be correct in the intended sense, but it would be even more vague for general use than our previous pair. In any event, the "non-human" man, the "non-natural nature" and the barely glimpsed structure of the future culture are inextricably bound together.

The coming order by which man will be related to his own works differs radically from the older one. It lacks the precise elements which constituted a culture in the older sense: the feeling of a tranquil fertility, of a flowering, beneficent realm. The new culture will be incomparably more harsh and more intense. It will lack the organic both in its sense of growth and of proportions; for the new culture will have been willed into being by the spirit of man, built up abstractly by his own hands. The new culture does not promise that breath necessary for a secure life and free growth; on the contrary it presents a vision of factories and barracks to the eyes of the mind.

A single fact, we must emphasize, will stamp the new culture: danger. Previously the simplest need for, and meaning of, culture has always been that culture created security. The experience of the earliest ages teaches us that when man can only see himself as surrounded by nature, he neither understands himself nor has he come to terms with his environment. At the dawn of civilization, the order of culture held back the encroaching powers of nature, thus making possible man's very life. As time moved on man gained a measure of security. Nature lost its alien or dangerous character and became a spring of inexhaustible plenitude and never-failing rejuvenation. This primitive source of perfections was what modern man found in nature. Today the situation is being reversed. The course of history has again led man into danger, but the danger confronting man today arises from within culture itself. From the efforts he expended and from the fortresses he built to conquer that ancient danger, man has created new dangers.

This pervasive threat does not originate in any of the particular difficulties facing man today, nor does it allow that science and technology can yet cope with it. The new danger arises from a factor intrinsic to the work of man, even to the work of his spirit.

The new danger arises from the factor of power.

To exercise power means, to a degree at least, that one has mastered "the given." Power over "the given" means that man has succeeded in checking those existential forces which oppose his life, that he has bent them to his will. Today the scepter of power is wielded by the hand of man. He has extensively mastered the immediate forces of nature, but he has not mastered the mediate forces because he has not yet brought under control his own native powers. Man today holds power over things, but we can assert confidently that he does not yet have power over his own power.

Man is free; he can use his power as he pleases. Within his very freedom reside the possibilities of misuse, a "misuse" which is one with destruction and with evil. What can guarantee man's proper use of his power in the realm of freedom? Nothing. There is no guarantee that man will use his freedom for the good; at best we could have the mere probability that he would use it for the good. We have mentioned already that even a prejudiced observer must conclude that man lacks today that rectified character which would ensure his right use of power. As yet he has not developed thoughtfully that ethic which would be effective for controlling the use of power. Moreover, no proper training ground now exists for such an ethic, either with the elite or among the masses.

And so it is that the dangers facing human freedom mount ominously day by day. Science and technology have so mastered the forces of nature that destruction, either chronic or acute and incalculable in extent, is now a possibility. Without exaggeration one can say that a new era of history has been born. Now and forever man will live at the brink of an ever-growing danger which shall leave its mark upon his entire existence.

One readily sees how little man today is prepared to take charge of this awful inheritance of power acquired up to the present moment, when one adds to these dangers the lulling sense of security for all with which man now accepts the current power culture. And the situation may well overwhelm humanity, not merely its weaker members but precisely those most active, its organizers, its leaders, its conquerors. During this century we have witnessed the first monstrous instances. It seems that too few people really understood the events of these years. Again and again one is haunted by the fear that in the final analysis only violence will be used in an effort to solve the flood of problems which threaten to engulf humanity. Should this inference prove to be true, it will mean that the false use of power in the conduct of human affairs has become the rule rather than the exception.

At the center of the endeavors of the coming culture will loom this problem of power. The solution of it will remain crucial. Every decision faced by the future age—those determining the welfare or misery of humanity and those determining the life or death of mankind itself—will be decisions centered upon the problem of power. Although it will increase automatically as time moves on, the concern will not be its increase but first the restraint and then the proper use of power.

The wildernesses of nature have long been under

the control of man; nature as it exists round and about us obeys its master. Nature now, however, has emerged once again into history from within the very depths of culture itself. Nature is rising up in that very form which subdued the wilderness—in the form of power itself. All the abysses of primeval ages yawn before man, all the wild choking growth of the long-dead forests press forward from this second wilderness, all the monsters of the desert wastes, all the horrors of darkness are once more upon man. He stands again before chaos, a chaos more dreadful than the first because most men go their own complacent ways without seeing, because scientifically-educated gentlemen everywhere deliver their speeches as always, because the machines are running on schedule and because the authorities function as usual.

Perhaps our hesitation in using the term "non-cultural culture" can now be better understood. If man's past achievements grew out of his culture, if the world he lived in was his culture, it becomes obvious that men today are not engaged in building a culture. They work for altogether different ends. The existential space occupied by the world of the present is not that of the old "culture"; the character of the coming world and of all that will depend upon it is not at all what man formerly knew as "culture."

Supporting the new order must be the root virtues of earnestness and gravity, both grounded in the truth. The objectivity with which so many issues are faced today is perhaps a way of nourishing these necessary virtues. For earnestness must will to know what is really at stake; it must brush aside empty rhetoric extolling progress or the conquest of nature; it must face heroically the duties forced upon man by his new situation.

The virtue of gravity will be spiritual, a personal courage devoid of the pathetic, a courage opposed to the looming chaos. This gravity or courage must be purer and stronger even than the courage man needs to face either atom bombs or bacteriological warfare, because it must restrain the chaos rising out of the very works of man. Finally it will find itself—as true courage always does—opposed by an enemy, the mass, ranged against it in public organizations clotted with catchwords.

Still we must add a third virtue: asceticism. The modern era rebelled against asceticism with every fiber of itself because it saw in asceticism the quintessence of all from which it wished to be free. It was this shrinking horror asceticism which lulled the modern world to sleep, which sapped its strength. Man must learn again to become a true master by conquering and by humbling himself. In no other way will he achieve the lordship of his own power. Only the freedom won through self-mastery can address itself with earnestness and gravity to those decisions which will affect all reality. These virtues today, however, look like metaphysical caricatures which busy themselves with trifles. The new freedom must seek a naked bravery, a genuine courage to unmask the fake heroisms for which contemporary man offers himself as sacrifice through his slavery to apparent absolutes.

These deep virtues could breed a spiritual art of government through which man could exercise power over power, through which he could distinguish right from wrong and ends from means. That government would truly measure human dignity and make room even under the strain of labor and battle for man himself to live in dignity and joy. Such a government would be an art, would indeed be *power*.

I have reiterated that I am no advocate of pessimism; it would be clearer to say that I am no advocate of a false pessimism, for there is a valid pessimism without which nothing great is ever achieved. This bitter urging enables the courageous heart and the creative spirit to persevere in all worthy ventures. It must assume its key position in the new world picture; it alone can predict the one decision which hovers within each of the advancing crises of our time. The alternative is ruin. Contemporary man can bring himself to destruction of both the interior and exterior orders or he can fashion a new universal order, a space where he could fit himself and, conscious of human dignity, lay the roadway of the future.

We cannot penetrate the questions now which ask about the nature, structure and character of this new universal order. Much could be implied about it by defining certain tendencies apparent in many places today: the growth of typical areas or forms of society, the real attitudes and motives of the new man. Such investigations, arduous in themselves, would exceed the bounds of this brief essay, however, and must be reserved for another study.

[V]

Always bearing in mind the reservations dictated by the nature of our meditation at large, we are now in a position to extend our observations into the religious character of the future order. First let us take a backward glance again.

During the Middle Ages life was interwoven with religion at every level and in every ramification. For all men the Christian Faith represented the generally-accepted truth. In some manner everything was stamped by Christianity and the Church: the social order, legislation, the ethos governing public and private life, the speculations of philosophy, artistic endeavors and the historic climate within which all ideas moved. Even while including all these things, we do not begin to indicate the cultural values won for the personality of man through this mingling of the cultural and the religious. Even injustice itself stood measured and condemned by Christianity. Although the Church had grown up in intimate union with the State, although Emperor and Pope or Prince and Bishop were often at odds—accusing and heaping abuse upon one another—men never questioned the Church herself.[4]

In time, man began to doubt the truth of Christian Revelation, and the doubt deepened as the medieval period drew toward its end. As an absolute standard claiming the right to measure the direction and conduct of human life, Revelation was enduring more and more vigorous attack. The new culture taking shape in Europe bred an outlook which thrust into prominence the increasing opposition to the Church. European man was adopting as self-evident truth the point of view which gave to politics, economics, government, science, art, philosophy and education principles and criteria immanent to themselves. In doing so men planted the seeds of non-Christian, even anti-Christian, ways of life in the soil of Europe. The old insistence that life be ordered by Revelation was taken as an encroachment by the Church, so completely had the new mind seized the power over men's imaginations. Even the faithful came to accept this state of affairs, accepting as normal the new order which said that matters of religion belonged in one sphere of life and secular matters in another. The individual man was left adrift to decide to what extent he would live in both of them.

As a consequence an autonomous secular order came into existence, uninfluenced by any direct Christian principles, while a new Christian order grew up by imitating the secular bent toward "autonomy" to a remarkable degree. In a parallel manner, science developed as pure science, economics as pure economics, politics as pure politics; similarly a religious religiosity was developed. Religion increasingly lost direct contact with the realities of life as it emptied itself of the secular and limited itself to "purely religious" doctrine and practice. For many men religion retained significance only in its formal aspects—in dedicating or sanctifying the crucial events of life such as birth or marriage or death.[5]

At many points in our study we have noted how this non-Christian culture commenced its growth at the very outset of the modern age. At first, the attack upon Christianity was directed against the content of Revelation. It was not made against those ethical values, individual or social, which had been perfected under the inspiration of the Faith. At the same time modern culture claimed those very values as its own foundation. Due largely to its changes in historic study, the modern world dedicated itself to the theory that it had discovered and developed ethical values. It is true, indeed, that the modern age did further the intrinsic worth of personality, of individual freedom, of responsibility and dignity, of man's inherent potentiality for mutual respect and help. These human values began their development, however, during earliest Christian times, while the Middle Ages continued their nurture by its cultivation of the interior and religious life. But the modern era suffered the invasion of consciousness by personal autonomy; human perfection became a cultural acquisition independent of ethics or of Christianity. This point of view was expressed in many ways by many groups, pre-eminently in the voicing of "the Rights of Man" during the French Revolution.

In truth, all human values find their root in Revelation; everything immediately human is related uniquely to Revelation. Man is related to God through Faith, but Faith is the effect of divine grace freely given and it draws the substance of all things human into itself. As a result, a Christian Order of life could come into existence in which "natural" human powers would be freed for full development, a development impossible outside a Christian Order. Man might then become conscious of values which, although evident in themselves, only take on visible manifestation under the *aegis* of Revelation. Those who maintain that these values and cultural attitudes are simply one with the autonomous development of human nature misunderstand the essential role of a Christian economy of Revelation, Faith and Grace. In fact the misunderstanding leads—permit me to speak plainly—to a kind of dishonesty which, as anyone who takes a clear-eyed view can see, is integral to the contemporary world itself.

Personality *is* essential to man. This truth becomes clear, however, and can be affirmed only under the guidance of Revelation, which related man to a living, personal God, which makes him a son of God, which teaches the ordering of His Providence. When man fails to ground his personal perfection in Divine Revelation, he still retains an awareness of the individual as a rounded, dignified and creative human being. He can have no consciousness, however, of the real person who is the absolute ground of each man, an absolute ground superior to every psychological or cultural advantage or achievement. The knowledge of what it means to be a person is inextricably bound up with the Faith of Christianity. An affirmation and a cultivation of the personal can endure for a time perhaps after Faith has been extinguished, but gradually they too will be lost.

A similar loss reveals itself in contemporary man's feeling that personal values inhere in special talents or social position. Gone is that reverence toward the person *qua* person, toward his qualitative uniqueness which cannot be conceptualized or repressed for any man even if he has been typed and measured in every other respect. A kindred loss is found in the exercise of human freedom. Instead of allowing for the full development of the existent self, freedom has been restricted to the psychological advantage or social privilege; it has ignored man's right to choose, to possess his own act while possessing himself in that act. As well, human love has been stifled, resting content with sympathy, a willingness to serve or with social duties, but seldom affirming the "thou" of the other even as it must accept the obligations of an "I." Not one of these attitudes can be viable, unless the Christian concept of the person is vigorously maintained. As soon as the true value of the person is lost, as soon as the Christian faith in the God-man relationship pales, all related attitudes and values begin to disappear.

Modern man's dishonesty was rooted in his refusal to recognize Christianity's affirmation of the God-man relationship. Even as the modern world acclaimed the worth of personality and of an order of personal values, it did away with their guarantor, Christian Revelation. This parallel affirmation and negation can be illustrated in modern history in the case of German classicism. Carried forward by truncated attitudes and values, German classicism was noble, humane and beautiful, but it lacked the final depth of truth. It had denied Revelation although it drew everywhere upon its effects. By the next generation the classical attitude toward man had also begun to fade, not because that generation did not occupy an equally high plane, but because an uprooted personal culture is powerless against the breakthrough of positivism. Thus the process of dissolution gained momentum. Suddenly the "value system" of the last two decades broke into history. In its sweeping contradiction of the whole modern tradition it proved that culture to have been only an apparent culture. That vacuum, however, had been created long before; now it was made evident to all men. With the denial of Christian Revelation genuine personality had disappeared from the human consciousness. With it had gone that realm of attitudes and values which only it can subsume.

The coming era will bring a frightful yet salutary preciseness to these conditions. No Christian can welcome the advent of a radical un-Christianity. Since Revelation is not a subjective experience but a simple Truth promulgated by Him Who also made the world, every moment of history which excludes that Revelation is threatened in its most hidden recesses. Yet it is good that modern dishonesty was unmasked. As the benefits of Revelation disappear even more from the coming world, man will truly learn what it means to be cut off from Revelation.

The question of the temper of the religious sensibility of the new age remains before us. Although the content of Revelation is eternal, its historical realization, its incarnation in man, varies with the passage of time. We could offer many implications about the religious temper of the new man, but it is necessary to restrict our meditations.

The rapid advance of a non-Christian ethos, however, will be crucial for the Christian sensibility. As unbelievers deny Revelation more decisively, as they put their denial into more consistent practice, it will become the more evident what it really means to be a Christian. At the same time, the unbeliever will emerge from the fogs of secularism. He will cease to reap benefit from the values and forces developed by the very Revelation he denies. He must learn to exist honestly without Christ and without the God revealed through Him; he will have to learn to experience what this honesty means. Nietzsche has already warned us that the non-Christian of the modern world had no realization of what it truly meant to be without Christ. The last decades have suggested what life without Christ really is. The last decades were only the beginning.

A new paganism differing from that of earlier ages will appear in the new world. Again contemporary man labors under illusory attitudes. In many cases, the non-Christian today cherishes the opinion that he can erase Christianity by seeking a new religious path, by returning to classical antiquity from which he can make a new departure. He is mistaken. No man can retrace history. As a form of historic existence classical antiquity is forever gone. When contemporary man becomes a pagan he does so in a way completely other than that of the pre-Christian. Even at the height of their cultural achievement the religious attitudes of the ancients were youthful and naive. Classical man only lived before that crisis which was the coming of Christ. With the advent of Christ man confronted a decision which placed him on a new level of existence. Sören Kierkegaard made this fact clear, once and for all. With the coming of Christ man's existence took on an earnestness which classical antiquity never knew simply because it had no way of knowing it. This earnestness did not spring from a human maturity; it sprang from the call which each person received from God through Christ. With this call the person opened his eyes, he was awakened for the first time in his life. This the Christian is whether he wills it or not. This earnestness prevailed, springing from the historic realization of the centuries that Christ is Being. It springs from man's common experience, frightful in its clarity, that He "knew what is in man," from the awareness in men of all the ages of that superhuman courage with which He mastered existence. When men deny this awareness we gain an impression that they suffer an immaturity, one common to the anti-Christian faiths of the ancient world.

Just as the renewal of the ancient classic myths against early Christianity was lifeless, so was the attempted rejuvenation of the Nordic myths. Seldom was either of those renewals the camouflage for a drive for power as it was with National Socialism.

Nordic paganism had existed prior to the decision man had to make before God's call through Christ, as had classical paganism. On the other hand, which ever way contemporary man decides, he must enter the depths of the person as revealed in Christ, leaving behind the secure but static life of immediate existence with its false rhythms and images.

This exact judgment must be made against all those attempts which would create a new myth through secular affirmation of the true Christian vision. Consider what happened in the later poetry of Rilke for instance. Basic to Rilke's[6] poetry is the will to shed the transcendence of Revelation and to ground existence absolutely on earth. Rilke's desire reveals its utter powerlessness when we note its total lack of harmony with the world now dawning. His attempts to adjust himself to the new world have a moving helplessness in a poem like the *"Sonnette an Orpheus,"* an alienating helplessness in the *"Elegien."* In respect to French existentialism, too, its negation of an intelligible existence is so violent that it seems to be an especially despairing kind of Romanticism made possible by the convulsions of the last decades.

A totally different realism would be needed to maneuver human attitudes before they could contradict Christian Revelation or build a fortress out of the world fully independent of Revelation. It remains to be seen to what extent the East can develop this other realism and to what exigencies man will be subjected as a consequence.

The Faith of Christian men will need to take on a

new decisiveness. It must strip itself of all secularism, all analogies with the secular world, all flabbiness and eclectic mixtures. Here, it seems to me, we have solid reasons for confidence. The Christian has always found it difficult to come to an understanding of modern attitudes, but we touch an issue here which needs more exact consideration. We do not mean that the Middle Ages was an historic epoch fully Christian in nature, nor do we mean that the modern world was an age fully un-Christian. Such assertions would resemble those of Romanticism, which have caused enough confusion. The Middle Ages were carried forward by forms of sensibility, thought and action which were basically neutral to the question of Faith, insofar as one can say such a thing at all. Similarly the modern world was carried by neutral forms. Within the modern era Western man created as his own an attitude of individual independence, yet that attitude said nothing about either the moral or the religious use which he made of his independence.

To be a Christian, however, demands an attitude toward Revelation; this demand can be found in every era of Western history. As far as this Christian attitude was concerned, Revelation remained equally near and equally distant for each epoch. Thus the Middle Ages contained its share of unbelief at every stage of decision; similarly the modern world demonstrated its share of full Christian affirmation. The modern Christian differed in character from his medieval ancestor, since he was forced to incarnate his faith within an historic situation which espoused individual independence, but he often succeeded as well as did the man of the Middle Ages. Indeed, the modern Christian faced obstacles which made it difficult for him to accept his age in the simple way that the medieval Christian could accept his. The memory of the revolt made against God by the modern world was too vividly impressed on the modern Christian. He was too aware of the manner in which his age had forced all cultural values to contradict his Faith. He knew too well the dubious and inferior position into which the world had forced that Faith. Besides these indignities there remained that modern dishonesty of which we have spoken, that hypocrisy which denied Christian doctrine and a Christian order of life even as it usurped its human and cultural effects. This dishonesty made the Christian feel insecure in his relation to the modern age. Everywhere within the modern world he found ideas and values whose Christian origin was clear, but which were declared the common property of all. How could he trust a situation like that? But the new age will do away with these ambivalences; the new age will declare that the secularized facets of Christianity are sentimentalities. This declaration will clear the air. The world to come will be filled with animosity and danger, but it will be a world open and clean.[7] This danger within the new world will also have its cleansing effect upon the new Christian attitude, which in a special way must possess both trust and courage.

Men have often said that Christianity is a refuge from the realities of the modern world, and this charge contains a good measure of truth, not only because dogma fixes the thought of a Christian on an objective, timeless order and creates a life which survives the passing of the ages but also because the Church has preserved a full cultural tradition which would otherwise have died. The world to come will present less basis for objecting to Christianity as a refuge.

The cultural deposit preserved by the Church thus far will not be able to endure against the general decay of tradition. Even when it does endure it will be shaken and threatened on all sides. Dogma in its very nature, however, surmounts the march of time because it is rooted in eternity, and we can surmise that the character and conduct of coming Christian life will reveal itself especially through its old dogmatic roots. Christianity will once again need to prove itself deliberately as a faith which is not self-evident; it will be forced to distinguish itself more sharply from a dominantly non-Christian ethos. At that juncture the theological significance of dogma will begin a fresh advance; similarly will its practical and existential significance increase. I need not say that I imply no "modernization" here, no weakening of the content or of the effectiveness of Christian dogma; rather I emphasize its absoluteness, its unconditional demands and affirmations. These will be accentuated. The absolute experiencing of dogma will, I believe, make men feel more sharply the direction of life and the meaning of existence itself.

In this manner, the Faith will maintain itself against animosity and danger. At the forefront of Christian life, man's obedience to God will assert itself with a new power. Knowing that the very last thing is at stake, that he has reached that extremity which only obedience could meet—not because man might become *heteronom*[8] but because God is Holy and Absolute—man will practice a pure obedience. Christianity will arm itself for an illiberal stand directed unconditionally toward Him Who is Unconditioned. Its illiberalism will differ from every form of violence, however, because it will be an act of freedom, an unconditional obedience to God; nor will it resemble an act of surrender to physical or psychic powers which might command one. No, man's unconditional answer to the call of God assumes within that very act the unconditional quality of the demand which God makes of him and which necessitates maturity of judgment, freedom and choice.

Here too we dare to hope. This trust is not based at all upon an optimism or confidence either in a universal order of reason or in a benevolent principle inherent to nature. It is based in God Who really is, Who alone is efficacious in His Action. It is based in this simple trust: that God is a God Who acts and Who everywhere prevails.

If I am right in my conclusions about the coming world, the Old Testament will take on a new significance. The Old Testament reveals the Living God Who smashes the mythical bonds of the earth, Who casts down the powers and the pagan rulers of life; it shows us the man of faith who is obedient to the acts of God according to the terms of the Covenant. These

Old Testament truths will grow in meaning and import. The stronger the demonic powers the more crucial will be that "victory over the world" realized in freedom and through Faith. It will be realized in the harmony between man's freedom freely returned to God from Whose own Creative Freedom it was gained. This will make possible not only effective action but even action itself. It is a strange thing that we should glimpse this holy way, this divine possibility, rising out of the very midst of universal power as it increases day by day.

This free union of the human person with the Absolute through unconditional freedom will enable the faithful to stand firm—God-centered—even though placeless and unprotected. It will enable man to enter into an immediate relationship with God which will cut through all force and danger. It will permit him to remain a vital person within the mounting loneliness of the future, a loneliness experienced in the very midst of the masses and all their organizations.

If we understand the eschatological text of Holy Writ correctly, trust and courage will totally form the character of the last age. The surrounding "Christian" culture and the traditions supported by it will lose their effectiveness. That loss will belong to the danger given by scandal, that danger of which it is said: "it will, if possible, deceive even the elect" (Matthew xxiv, 24).

Loneliness in faith will be terrible. Love will disappear from the face of the public world (Matthew xxiii, 12), but the more precious will that love be which flows from one lonely person to another, involving a courage of the heart born from the immediacy of the love of God as it was made known in Christ. Perhaps man will come to experience this love anew, to taste the sovereignty of its origin, to know its independence of the world, to sense the mystery of its final why? Perhaps love will achieve an intimacy and harmony never known to this day. Perhaps it will gain what lies hidden in the key words of the providential message of Jesus: that things are transformed for the man who makes God's Will for His Kingdom his first concern (Matthew vi, 33).

These eschatological conditions will show themselves, it seems to me, in the religious temper of the future. With these words I proclaim no facile apocalyptic. No man has the right to say that the End is here, for Christ Himself has declared that only the Father knows the day and the hour (Matthew xxiv, 36). If we speak here of the nearness of the End, we do not mean nearness in the sense of time, but nearness as it pertains to the essence of the End, for in essence man's existence is now nearing an absolute decision. Each and every consequence of that decision bears within it the greatest potentiality and the most extreme danger.

NOTES

1. Guardini is referring to the world-wide Goethe Bicentennial.—Ed.

2. The expression "non-human" is quite inappropriate, and the reactions to both the first editions of this work justified my fear that the term would be taken to mean the "inhuman." I can find no better term, however, and

I can only ask the reader to understand it as it is used in the exposition of my thesis.

3. The endeavor here involved may be an approach to an abstract art, insofar as abstract art is really "art" and not simply naked experimentation or distorted reproduction.

4. Here we must make a necessary distinction. The Christian Faith is a bond linking man to the God of Revelation. The perfection of Faith is measured by the clarity with which this bond is seen and by the loyalty with which it is maintained. To experience religion *per se* is another question, regardless of the vitality with which a man senses his relation to the Divine or of the degree to which it affects his life. During the medieval period man possessed a natural disposition to receive the imprint of the Divine which was markedly high. Religious experience was a reality, strong, deep, and delicately developed. Religious values permeated all things, every facet of life. Poetry and art, government, forms of society and economy, customs, myths and legends—even apart from their content—teach us about the religious character of all existence. In its religious consciousness, the Middle Ages was linked intimately with classic antiquity, despite the profound changes which the vitality of the Nordic races had brought to medieval Christendom as the great migrations flowed over Europe. From its outset the medieval capacity for religious experience was different from Christian piety *per se;* similarly, the European view of reality, of things and events, was different from the content of Revelation. Yet the two spheres of experience were definitely related. Natural religious experience was purified by Revelation, taken into it, receiving thereby new significance. At the same time, the capacity for natural religious experience brought to Christian Faith the elemental stuff and power out of which a world and a way of life were brought into being, through which the content of Revelation was made compatible with terrestrial realities.

5. These developments have their contemporary significance, too, which we note in addressing ourselves to the religious situation of the modern era. And there is also another pertinent consideration: the loss of that openness toward the religious itself of which we have already spoken.

The modern era experienced the increasing penetration of nature by rational and experimental techniques. It came to see politics as the mere play of power for the sake of naked interest; it saw economics develop as a discipline gauged to a logic inherent within utility and welfare. The modern era grasped technology as a gigantic apparatus available for any purpose man might conceive. Art became the mere fashioning of forms out of matter according to strict aesthetic criteria. Pedagogy became an instrument with which the teacher produced the kind of men needed to support the status quo and the accepted culture. To the very extent that the new ideal was actualized, the natural ability to open oneself to religious experience waned. By religious openness, we repeat, we do not mean the Faith and its content of Christian Revelation nor a life determined by them. We mean that immediate interest, rather, in the religious *per se* which is present in all. We mean a concern for, and an ability to be gripped by, those mysterious currents which run throughout the world and reveal themselves to all peoples at all times. To a considerable extent, however, modern man lost both his belief in the Revelation of Christ and this latter ability to experience his world in a religious way. His world had become a "thing" increasingly profane. This impoverishment of the religious sensibility was to have far-reaching effect.

For example, consider that the tapestry of events making up the life of a man was no longer seen as the working of that Providence of which Jesus spoke. It was not even thought to be the work of that mysterious fate which led the life of classical man. In its varied relations, in its *over-all* pattern, life was reduced to a mere sequence of empirical causes and effects, which, since intelligible to man, could be guided by him. Emptied of the religious, this outlook is expressed today variously. One example can be taken as typical—the present system of insurance. If we look at the extreme development and spreading of insurance promotion today throughout many lands, it appears as a system stripped of all religious base. It "provides for" all eventualities and renders them harmless merely by charting their frequency and importance.

The crucial events of the life of man—conception, birth, sickness, death—have lost their mystery. They have become biological or social phenomena dealt with more and more by a medical science or by a series of techniques which claim an increasing confidence in their own efficacy. Insofar as the great crises in human life could reveal truths which cannot be mastered by modern techniques, they are "anaesthetized" and thus rendered irrelevant. In this connection, we cannot avoid thinking of those auxiliary techniques for the rational conquest of sickness or death which appear today not only at the horizons of our culture but also at its very center, techniques which would remove lives no longer of service to "life" itself, no longer corresponding to the ends of the state.

The state once possessed a religious significance, a majesty which sprang from its dedication to the divine. All of that withered; today it has disappeared. Then, the modern state was thought to derive its power from the people; for a time efforts were made to transfer the old sense of majesty to the people themselves. Note in this regard, the theories of the Romantics, the theories behind nationalism, behind the earlier democracies. But the "majesty of the people" was soon emptied of any positive content; it came to mean that the "people" were the multitudes who belonged to the state. In some manner, the state came to express their will, but quickly it incarnated the many in the execution of its own measures and only for so long as the state itself was not mastered by a powerful or militant minority. Many things could be said in this connection, but let us be content with indicating that the forms of human existence under the state were derived exclusively from the empirical order.

Is it possible to build a life for man or for society upon exclusively empirical grounds, a life which could endure? Could such a life foster the values and insights necessary to remain truly human? Could it even reach the goals which it seeks?

Is not every order of being sapped of strength when taken in a merely empirical way? For example, the state demands the oath, the most binding of all contracts, in which a man guarantees his avowal with a pledge or obliges himself to an action by referring his declaration expressly and solemnly to God Himself. What happens to the oath when it loses this reference to God? (And we must admit that recent usage tends to strip the oath of divine reference.) It becomes a mere declaration: the man swearing admits that he is aware that he will be imprisoned if he does not tell the truth. This formula makes little sense and cannot be effective.

Every being is more than itself. Every event points beyond a bare formal completion of its own act. All things are related to a reality above and beyond themselves; from this reference alone can they be perfected and carried to fulfillment. Failing their reference to the Other, all things, all orders of reality become empty shells. Stripped of their significance, they can convince no one of their root value. The law of the state is more than a set of rules governing human behavior; behind it exists something untouchable, and when a law is broken it makes its impact on the conscience of man. Social order is more than a warrant against friction, than a guarantee for the free exercise of communal life; behind it stands something which makes an injury against society a crime. This religious dimension of law suffuses the entire moral order. It gives to ethical action, that is action necessary for the very existence of man, its own proper norms, which it executes from without and without pressure. Only the religious element of law guarantees the unity and cooperation of the whole order of human behavior.

No such thing as a merely worldly world exists even when the stubborn will seems to have fashioned a strictly secular order, for it has made an order which cannot function. It has produced an unsuccessful, an unconvincing artifact. The living intuition of man the person, lying beyond and under all rationalistic thought, cannot be convinced by a secular world. His heart cannot feel that such a world pays.

Without religion life becomes like a machine without oil; it runs hot; even if it functions, some part of it is always burning out. One after another its varied parts which ought to fit together exactly are immobilized. Just as the center of action is lost, its cohesion is prevented. Existence has lost its order. Finally, the engine of society breaks down, just as it has been short circuited during the past thirty years by the increasing loss of social contacts. Obsessed with the exercise of his own power, man today frantically hunts for a way out of his own social breakdown. As long as men are unable to control themselves from within, however, they will inevitably be "organized" by forces from without. To ensure proper, external function the state steps in and places, that is it forces, its own power upon a new order. But, we ask, is it possible for man as man to continue to exist under the naked use of power itself?

6. I hope to be able to present more exact information on this issue in a complete interpretation of the "Daineser Elegien."

7. What we noted earlier concerning the decline of primitive religious sensibility, of the ability to infuse all things with a sense of the religious, will increase in the new era. A fullness of religious sensibility helps faith, but it can also veil and secularize its content. If this fullness diminishes, faith becomes leaner but purer and stronger. The new Faith will therefore open itself to what is genuinely real; its center of gravity will descend more deeply into the personal; it will affect all things with decision, loyalty and self-conquest.

8. We retain Guardini's usage of the Greek *heteronom*. The English derivative would probably be "heteronomous," meaning: not self-governing or not self-determining, *etc.*—Ed.

II.

POWER AND RESPONSIBILITY

A Course of Action for the New Age

CHAPTER FOUR

THE ESSENCE OF POWER

INTRODUCTION

Since every historical epoch encompasses the whole range of human experience, its character may be determined by any aspect of that experience. Yet in the course of history now one, now another element of existence seems to acquire special significance.

Thus we might say the ultimate goal of antiquity was to find the model of the well-formed man and the noble work, and the result of men's striving in that direction was what we mean today by the concept "classical."

The Middle Ages experienced with particular force man's relation to the transcendent God, and in that experience the upsurging strength of the young peoples of the West awoke. From its new vantage-point "above" the world, the will now sought to shape the world, and that unique combination of ardor and architectural precision so characteristic of the medieval conception of life came into being.

Finally, the modern age, with intellect and technique in hitherto unknown proximity to material reality, grasps at the world. What determines its sense of existence is power over nature. In ever swifter advance—exploring, planning, constructing—man takes things into his possession.

Today the modern age is essentially over. The chains of cause and effect that it established will of course continue to hold. Historical epochs are not neatly severed like the steps of a laboratory experiment. While one era prevails, its successor is already forming, and its predecessor continues to exert influence for a long time. To this day we find elements of a still-vital antiquity in southern Europe, and we run across strong medieval currents in many places. Thus in the yet nameless epoch which we feel breaking in on us from all sides, the last consequences of the modern age are still being drawn, although that which determined the essence of that age no longer determines the character of the historical epoch now beginning.

Everywhere man's power is in unbroken ascendancy. Indeed, we might contend that his power has only now entered upon its critical stage. Nevertheless, essentially, the will of the age is no longer directed to the augmenting of power as such. The modern age considered every increase in intellectual-technical power an unquestionable gain, fervently believing all such increase to be progress, progress in the direction of a decisive fulfillment of the supreme meaning and value of existence. Today this belief is growing shaky, a condition which in itself indicates the beginning of a new epoch. We no longer believe that increase of power is necessarily the same thing as increase of value. Power has grown questionable. And not merely from the standpoint of a cultural critique (like that which opposed the prevailing optimism of the nineteenth century, especially toward its end), but fundamentally questionable. Into the public consciousness creeps the suspicion that our whole attitude to power is wrong; more, that our growing power is a growing threat to ourselves. That threat finds its expression in the nuclear bomb, which has captured the vital awareness and imagination of the public and become the symbol of something fraught with more general meaning.

In the coming epoch, the essential problem will no longer be that of increasing power—though power will continue to increase at an ever swifter tempo—but of curbing it. The core of the new epoch's intellectual task will be to integrate power into life in such a way that man can employ power without forfeiting his humanity. For he will have only two choices: to match the greatness of his power with the strength of his humanity, or to surrender his humanity to power and perish. The very fact that we can define these alternatives without seeming utopian or moralistic—because by so doing we but voice something of which the public is more or less aware—is a further indication that the new epoch is overtaking the old.

From the above, the direction of the following study is clear. It is the sequel to *The End of the Modern World*. In some places it presupposes what was said there; in others it develops it. The two skeins of thought crisscross again and again, necessitating certain repetitions. On the other hand, *Power and Responsibility* is complete in itself.

[I]

First of all, let us try to get a clear idea of what "power" is. May the word be applied to the immediate forces of nature? May we say, for instance, that a storm, an epidemic, a lion has power?

Obviously not, save in a fuzzy, metaphorical sense. In the natural forces we do of course have effective objects capable of producing specific results; but what is lacking is something we include involuntarily when we think of "power," namely, initiative. The things of nature have or are "energy," not power. Energy becomes power only when some consciousness recognizes it, some will capable of decision directs it toward specific goals. Only in one limited sense can we apply the word to natural energies: when we conceive of them as "powers"—in other words, as mysterious beings somehow endowed with personal initiative. However, this conception hardly fits our present-day picture of existence. It belongs rather to the mythical image of the world in which the essences of things act, meet, conflict with one another, or join forces. Such "powers" are of a religious nature, evolving more or less clearly as "the gods."

Related to this use of the word, though still cloudier, is its use in speaking of "the powers" of the heart, mind, and blood. Here again is an instance of originally mythical conceptions of divine or demonic initiatives at work in man's inner world independently of his will. Masquerading in scientific, aesthetic, sociological concepts, they stalk strangely unchallenged (hence all too effectively) through modern man's intellectual-spiritual household.[1]

On the other hand, does an idea have power? An ethical norm? We often say so, but erroneously. Ideas—norms as such—have validity, not power. They exist in unruffled objectivity. Their meaning shines out but is not yet, by itself, effective. Power is the ability to move reality. Alone, an idea cannot do this. It can and does become power when it is integrated into the concrete life of a man, when it becomes one with his development, instincts, emotions, with the tensions of his interior life, with his intentions, his work, and its requirements.

Hence we may speak of power in the true sense of the word only when two elements are present: real energies capable of changing the reality of things, of determining their condition and interrelations; and awareness of those energies, the will to establish specific goals and to launch and direct energies toward those goals.

All this presupposes spirit, that reality in man which renders him capable of extricating himself from the immediate context of nature in order to direct it in freedom.

[II]

To the essence of power as a specifically human phenomenon belongs its ability to give purpose to things.

By this we do not mean that the process of utilizing power is directed by a purpose; as much is true also of the processes of nature, in which nothing exists that is without purpose. In nature we have both the most elemental causality (no effect without due cause) and finality (each element of reality arranged in relation to part and whole), and out of these come those particular forms of pattern and function that we find in physical, chemical, and biological relationships. But our opening statement implies more: that the initiative which exercises power also establishes the purpose of that power.

Power awaits direction. Unlike the forces of nature, it becomes part of a cause-and-effect relationship, not through necessity, but only through the intervention of an agent. Solar energy, for example, automatically, brings about certain biological reactions in the plant: growth, coloration, metabolism, movement. But the forces which go into the making of a tool must be directed by the craftsman. They are at his disposal and he directs them—knowing, planning, shaping them—to the end for which he intends them.

This implies something more: when man's spirit is brought to bear upon the forces given by nature, an element of free choice enters the relationship. The spirit can direct them to whatever end it wills, and everything depends on whether this end is constructive or destructive, noble or base, good or evil.

In other words, there is no such thing as power that, in and of itself, is valuable or significant. Power receives its character only when someone becomes aware of it, determines its use, and puts it to work. This means that someone must answer for it.

There is no such thing as power that is not answered for. Natural energies need not be answered for—that is, to say it better, they exist not on the level of responsibility, but on that of natural necessity. Human power for which no one is answerable simply does not exist.[2] It results in action—or at least consent to action—and, as such, exists within the responsibility of a human authority, hence of some person. This is true even when the person responsible rejects responsibility.

Indeed, it continues to hold true even when human affairs are so deranged or falsely arranged that those responsible can no longer be named. When this happens, when to the question "Who did this?" neither "I" nor "we," neither a person nor a body of people replies, the exercise of power has apparently become a natural force. Precisely this seems to occur with growing frequency, for in the course of historical development, the bearers of power have become increasingly anonymous. The progressive nationalization of social, economic, technical processes, as well as the materialistic theories of history as necessity, signify the attempt of our time to destroy the character of responsibility, to divorce power from person, and to place its exercise on the level of natural forces.[3] In reality, the essential character of power as personally answerable energy can never be destroyed; it can only be corrupted—corruption which, becoming guilt, works itself out in destruction.[4]

In itself, power is neither good nor evil; its quality is determined by him who wields it. In fact, of itself it is only potentially constructive or destructive, since it is essentially governed by freedom. When power is not determined by freedom—that is to say, by the human will—either nothing happens at all, or there arises a hodgepodge of habits, incoherent impulses, and blind herd-instincts: chaos.

Thus power is as much a possibility for good and the positive as it is a threat of destruction and evil. The danger grows with the growth of power, a fact that is brought home to us today with brutal clarity. A more immediate danger threatens when power is at the disposal of a will that is either morally misguided or morally uncommitted. Or there may be no appealable will at all, no person answerable for power, only an anonymous organization, each department of which transfers its authority to the next, thus leaving each—seemingly—exempt from responsibility. This type of power becomes particularly ominous when, as is true so often these days, respect for the human person, for his dignity and responsibility, for his personal values of freedom and honor, for his initiative and way of life grow visibly feebler.

Then power acquires characteristics which ultimately only Revelation is in a position to interpret: it becomes demonic. Once action is no longer sustained by personal awareness, is no longer morally answerable, a peculiar vacancy appears in the actor. He no longer has the feeling that *he*, personally, is acting; that since the act originates with him he is responsible for it. He no longer seems master of the act; instead the act seems to pass through him, and he is left feeling like one element in a chain of events. And with others it is the same, so that there remains no real authority to appeal to, since authority presupposes a person whose warrant comes directly from God, to whom he is answerable. Instead, there is a growing sense of there being no one at all who acts, only a dumb, intangible, invisible, indefinable something which derides questioning. Its functions appear to be necessary, so the individual submits to them. Seemingly incomprehensible, it is simply accepted as a "mystery" (in reality it is only a pseudo-mystery) and as such draws to itself those sentiments, in distorted form, which a man is meant to reserve for his fate, not to say, God.[5]

This vacancy comes into being when the person— which, to be sure, can never be entirely lost, for a man can no more throw away his person than he can be deprived of it—is ignored, denied, violated. But the emptiness does not remain, for that would mean that the human being would somehow be reduced to a natural being, and his power to natural energy. This is impossible. What does happen is that the void is succeeded by a faithlessness which hardens to an attitude, and into this no man's land stalks another initiative, the demonic.

The nineteenth century, self-confident in its unshaken faith in progress, ridiculed the figure of "the demon," whom we shall name by his correct name, Satan. Those capable of insight do not laugh. They know that he exists, and actively so. Yet even our own more realistic age fails to face up to the truth about him. When it mentions, as it frequently does, "the demonic," it does not use the words seriously. Often they are just so much talk. Even when the speaker is sincere, "demonic" is simply his way of expressing a vague fear, or he means it psychologically, as a kind of symbol. When "religious science" and depth psychology, when press and screen and theater say "demonic," they are only admitting that there is an element of incomprehensible inconsistency in the world, of contradiction and malice. It is known to be extremely sinister, and man's reaction to it is a peculiar foreboding and fear. In certain individuals, as in particular historical situations, it comes powerfully to the fore. The truth behind it is not "the demonic," but Satan; and who that is, only Revelation can properly say.

[III]

Now for one last aspect of power: its universality. Man's power, the use of which is peculiarly satisfying, is not limited to any one "department" of his being isolated from the rest; it is related to his every activity and competence—or at least it can be related to them, including those which at first glance seem to have no connection with the nature of power.

It is clear that every act of doing and creating, of possessing and enjoying, produces an immediate sense of power. The same is true of all acts of the vitality. Any activity in which a man exercises his vitality directly is a power-exercise, and he will experience it as such.

Much the same may be said of knowledge, the perceptive and understanding penetration of that which is. In the act of knowing, the knower experiences the power that effects such penetration. He feels truth "dawn" on him, a sensation which is succeeded by that of having "grasped" it. Pride in his achievement follows, an elation which is the higher, the farther removed from everyday experience the truth he has mastered appears to be. Nietzsche refers to this as the pride of philosophers. Here obedience to truth turns into an affectation of mastery over truth, a kind of intellectual law-making.

Cognition's consciousness of power may also find

directly effective expression: namely, when it passes over into magic. Fairy tale and myth sing of knowledge which empowers. The hero who knows the name of a person or thing possesses power over it, "charm," "spell," "curse." In a very profound sense, the power of knowledge is recognition of the world's essence, of the hidden workings of destiny, of the passage of things human and divine. This is the knowledge by which "the gods of government" make themselves lords of the world; the knowledge by which Satan, in the story of the Fall, insinuates a false meaning into the words of God in order to blur the real distinction between good and evil. In fairy tales it is the secret word which overpowers the dragon, raises the sunken treasure, breaks the spell.

The sense of power can cling even to conditions which seem to contradict it: to suffering, privation, defeat. Thus, for example, the sufferer is convinced that he has reached a deeper understanding of life through his suffering than others enjoy; or the unsuccessful businessman assures himself that his higher ethical sense is what really prevented his success.

Even the torturous inferiority complex is always coupled with a more or less hidden presumption, if only that of insisting on goals far beyond normal reach.

Every act, every condition, indeed, even the simple fact of existing is directly or indirectly linked to the conscious exercise and enjoyment of power. In positive form, this provides a sense of self-reliance and strength; in the negative, it becomes arrogance, vanity, pride.

Consciousness of power has also a general, onto-logical aspect. It is a direct expression of existence, an expression which can turn to the positive or the negative, to truth or its semblance, to right or wrong.

With this, the phenomenon of power crosses over into the metaphysical, or to be precise, the religious.

NOTES

1. This is particularly evident in depth-psychology, some of whose concepts are amazingly suggestive of alchemy.

2. Modern thought has done much to becloud the whole subject of natural energies or forces. Actually, it has led thought back to the unclarity which Christian philosophy filtered out of Greek, particularly Hellenistic, thinking. Now again we hear phrases like "nature has so ordained" this or that, or such and such "is contrary to nature's intent." Such remarks are senseless. Nature does not intend anything. All we can truly say is that in its natural context, a thing must be thus or so. Anything more is lyricism—or disoriented mythology. In reality, the phrase "nature does" has usurped the former "God, the Creator of nature, has ordained" this or that. Thus ultimately, even the forces of nature are answered for—creatively, by God.

3. A phenomenon which also makes its appearance in our present development seems to contradict this tendency: dictatorship. Directly proportionate to the disappearance of responsibility is the appearance of false responsibility with its leaning to direct action by autocratic, or rather arbitrary, decisions. Look closely and you will discover that in the dictatorship, those held "responsible" are not really so at all, but are merely commandeered by higher "authorities" who supervise their every move. Even the "supreme authority" knows himself to be the mere executor of a mass-will. As soon as he proves unsatisfactory in this role, he is eliminated, even as he eliminated lesser "authorities" the moment they showed signs of personal initia-

tive. In other words, a dictator is only a "constructive" counter-weight to collectivism. Both together extinguish the person, setting up in his place the anonymous functionary.

4. With his concept of "guiltless action," Nietzsche also attempted to separate power from responsibility (which always is ethical responsibility) and to render it a high-level natural process. Compared with such power's unbroken strength, awareness of such responsibility was allegedly no more than a disease. In Nietzsche the shift is more subtle than in collectivism. Personal initiative is at first maintained, but the individual himself is "beyond good and evil," is pure, self-begotten, creative power. Thus as an individual he becomes a "nature" in which the energies of earth, world, and cosmos are effective. In reality, the individual is irrevocably *person* and, as such, is by nature morally responsible. Thus the alleged naturalness of Nietzsche's Superman is mere semblance—and desertion.

5. See Kafka's novels *The Trial* and *The Castle*.

CHAPTER FIVE

THE THEOLOGICAL CONCEPT OF POWER

[I]

As we have just seen, Revelation's testimony is essential to any deeper understanding of power.

The foundation of power is revealed at the beginning of the Old Testament in connection with man's essential destination. After the creation of the world is narrated, the first chapter of Genesis says: "And God said, Let us make man, wearing our own image and likeness; let us put him in command of the fishes in the sea, and all that flies through the air, and the cattle, and the whole earth, and all the creeping things that move on earth. So God made man in his own image, made him in the image of God. Man and woman both he created them. And God pronounced his blessing on them, Increase and multiply and fill the earth, and make it yours; take command of the fishes in the sea, and all that flies through the air, and all the living things that move on the earth."

Soon after, in the second chapter on creation, we find: "And now, from the clay of the ground, the Lord God formed man, breathed into his nostrils the breath of life, and made him a living soul." (Genesis i, 26-28; ii, 7)

First we are informed that man is a being different in kind from all other beings. Like all living
things, he was created, but in a special manner, in
the likeness of God. He is made of earth—the earth
of the fields that nourish him—but a whiff of the
spirit-breath of God animates him. Thus he is integrated into nature, yet at the same time through his
direct relation to God, he is able to confront nature.
He is in a position to rule the earth, and should do
so, even as he is meant to be fruitful and make it his
children's habitation.

Chapter Two goes on to develop man's relation to
the world from the standpoint we touched on a while
back: man is to be master not only of nature, but also
of himself; he is to have the strength necessary not only
for his tasks, but also to continue his own life—
through generation. "But the Lord God said, It is not
well that man should be without companionship; I will
give him a mate of his own kind. And now, from the
clay of the ground, all the wild beasts and all that flies
through the air were ready fashioned, and the Lord
God brought them to Adam, to see what he would call
them; the name Adam gave to each living creature is its
name still. Thus Adam gave names to all the cattle, and
all that flies in the air, and all the wild beasts; and still
Adam had no mate of his own kind." Man then must
know that he is essentially different from animals, that
therefore he can neither truly share his life nor gener-
ate new life with them. "So the Lord God made Adam
fall into a deep sleep, and, while he slept, took away
one of his ribs, and filled its place with flesh. This rib,

which he had taken out of Adam, the Lord God formed into a woman; and when he brought her to Adam, Adam said, Here, at last, is bone that comes from mine, flesh that comes from mine; it shall be called Woman, this thing that was taken out of Man. That is why a man is destined to leave father and mother, and cling to his wife instead, so that the two become one flesh." (Genesis ii, 18-20, 21-24)

These texts, which echo and reecho throughout the Old and New Testaments, clearly indicate that man was given power over nature and over his own life, power that imparts both the right and the obligation to rule.

Man's natural God-likeness consists in this capacity for power, in his ability to use it and in his resultant lordship. Herein lies the essential vocation and worth of human existence—Scripture's answer to the question: Where does the ontological nature of power come from? Man cannot be human and, as a kind of addition to his humanity, exercise or fail to exercise power; the exercise of power is essential to his humanity. To this end the Author of his existence determined him. We do well to remind ourselves that in the citizen of today, the agent of contemporary development, there is a fateful inclination to utilize power ever more completely, both scientifically and technically, yet not to acknowledge it, preferring to hide it behind aspects of "utility," "welfare," "progress," and so forth.[1] This is one reason why man governs without developing a corresponding ethos of government. Thus power has come to be exercised in a manner that is not ethically determined; the most telling expression of this is the anonymous business corporation.

Only when these facts have been accepted, does the phenomenon of power receive its full weight, its greatness, as well as its earnestness, which is grounded in responsibility. If human power and the lordship which stems from it are rooted in man's likeness to God, then power is not man's in his own right, autonomously, but only as a loan, in fief. Man is lord by the grace of God, and he must exercise his dominion responsibly, for he is answerable for it to him who is Lord by essence. Thus sovereignty becomes obedience, service.[2]

Service first of all, in the sense that sovereignty is to be exercised with respect for the truth of things. This is what is meant by the key passage in the second chapter on creation, which distinguishes man's essence from the animal's, explaining why communal life is possible for man only with his own kind, never for man and beast. Sovereignty, then, does not mean that man imposes his will on the gifts of nature, but that his possessing, sharing, making is done in acceptance of each thing's being what it is—an acceptance symbolized in the "name" by which he tries to express its essential quality. Sovereignty is obedience and service also in that it operates as part of God's creation, where its mission is to continue what God in his absolute freedom created as nature, to develop it on the human level of finite freedom as history and culture. Man's sovereignty is not meant to establish an independent world of man, but to complete the world of God as a free, human world in accordance with God's will.

[II]

Next we have the account of man's testing, and we see at once that it is the turning-point of his existence. What is tested is nothing less central than man's power and its use. The profundity of the account demands an almost word-for-word interpretation.

"So the Lord God took the man and put him in his garden of delight, to cultivate and tend it. And this was the command which the Lord God gave the man, Thou mayest eat thy fill of all the trees in the garden except the tree which brings knowledge of good and evil; if ever thou eatest of this, thy doom is death." (Genesis ii, 15-17)

The meaning of the passage becomes clear the moment we rid ourselves of the usual naturalistic interpretations. According to the first of these, "the tree which brings knowledge of good and evil" means man's freedom to distinguish between true and false, right and wrong—in other words, intellectual maturity in place of uncritical fancies and personal, childlike dependence. Another interpretation, closely related to the first, holds that the tree stands for sexual maturity—the fulfilment and self-realization of man and his mate through fruitfulness. All such interpretations are based strongly on the notion that man had to become guilty in order to become mature, critical, master of himself and things. Hence to commit evil was to break through to freedom.

We have only to read the text carefully to see that there is absolutely no substance for such "psychologistics." Nowhere is knowledge—still less, sexual maturity—withheld. On the contrary, man is meant explicitly to gain precisely these: freedom of knowledge, power over things, and the fulfilment of life. All are essential to him, expressly his by creation, both as gift and as obligation. He is to rule over the animals, which represent all natural things; to do so, he must know them. When the test comes, he has already accomplished this. He has recognized the essence of the animals and expressed it in their names. And how could sexual maturity possibly be forbidden, when it is said explicitly that man and wife are to be "one flesh" and to people the earth with their descendants?

All of this means that man is to attain sovereignty in the broadest sense of the word, but that this is possible only by maintaining his relationship of obedience to God, by remaining in His service. Man is to be lord of the earth by remaining an image of God, not by demanding identity with his Maker.

The following, which is basic to any interpretation of existence, shows how temptation sets in: "Of all the beasts which the Lord God had made, there was none that could match the serpent in cunning. It was he who said to the woman, What is this command God has given you, not to eat the fruit of any tree in the garden? To which the woman answered, We can eat the fruit of any tree in the garden except the tree in the middle of it; it is this God has forbidden us to eat or even to touch, on pain of death. And the serpent said to her, What is this talk of death? God knows well that as soon as you eat this fruit your eyes will be opened, and you yourselves will be like gods, knowing good and evil. And with that the woman, who saw that the fruit was good to eat, saw, too, how it was pleasant to look at and charmed the eye, took some fruit from the tree and ate it; and she gave some to her husband, and he ate with her. Then the eyes of both were opened, and they became aware of their nakedness; so they sewed fig-leaves together, and made themselves girdles." (Genesis iii, 1-7)

The serpent, a symbolical figure for Satan, confuses man by misrepresenting the fundamental facts of human existence: the essential difference between Creator and created; between Archetype and image; between self-realization through truth and through usurpation; between sovereignty in service and independent sovereignty. In the process, the clear concept of God is perverted to a myth. For to say God knows that man can become like him by doing the act he has forbidden is to imply that God is afraid, that he feels his divinity threatened by man, that his relation to man is that of a mythical divinity. "The gods" spring from the same natural root as man, hence ultimately are no more than he. They are lords only factiously, not essentially. Thus it is possible for man to dethrone them and set himself up as lord; he has only to discover the means. And the Tempter claims the means to be "the tree which brings knowledge of good and evil." This knowledge too he presents mythically, as the privileged initiation of the ruling lord of earth into the world-secret, which lends magical power and warrants lordship. Once men have this, they are a match for any god and can dethrone him. There is nothing of all this in the words of God. Satan tempts man by distorting the genuine God-man relation, placing it in a mythical twilight which falsifies it.[3]

To pass the test, man must honor God's truth and remain obedient to it. Instead, he falls into the trap and raises the claim to sovereignty by his own grace. And it is with truly apocalyptic power that we are told how disobedience brings, not knowledge that makes man a god, but the deadly experience of "nakedness" so essentially different from that mentioned at the beginning of the passage: "Both went naked...and thought it no shame."

With this event, man's fundamental relation to existence is destroyed. Now as before, he has power and is capable of ruling. But the order in which that sovereignty had meaning (as service answerable to him who is Sovereign by essence) is destroyed. Now dis-order reigns.

Thus, according to Biblical teaching, the pure phenomenon of power and the sovereignty stemming from it no longer exist. At the beginning of human history looms an event whose significance cannot be expressed in the simple concepts of inner or outward resistance, of disturbance and danger. Here is no case of inner-historical, biological, psychological, or spiritual damage. Nor is it a question of an ethical wrong invading the known structure of being from without. Here is an event which pursues history, forever disrupting man's relation to his Creator, the basis of human existence. Ever since, history takes its course in a world that is marked by disorder.

This is what makes the Biblical view of history unique. It contradicts both the natural-optimistic and the cultural-pessimistic interpretations of history which dominated the modern age—both of which, for all their abundance of material, methodical precision, and thoughtfulness, are unrealistic and thin. Space does not permit us to examine them in detail here. For this limited study the important point is that from the Fall on, power has received a new and far-reaching characteristic; now it possesses not only the possibility, but also the tendency (not to say the inevitable tendency) to abuse which is represented in the great mythological figures of *hybris* or pride—in Prometheus and Sisyphus. These are not myths of archetypal man, of man as such, any more than the Fall of man appertains to man as he was created. They are expressions of *fallen* man.[4]

What the Old Testament has to say on the subject of power is completed only in the Revelation of the New.

[III]

The content of the New Testament is not easily explained. The Old Testament's doctrine is one of noble simplicity. It has what might be called a classical quality, in which God's intention and man's resistance, creation's original circumstances and those resulting from revolt and the Fall, conflict dramatically. The presentation of the New Testament is much more difficult to understand.

Salvation is no mere improvement of the conditions of being, it ranks in importance with the creation of all being. It originates not within the structure of the world, not even in the most spiritual parts of it, but within the pure freedom of God. It is a new beginning, which provides a new platform for existence, a new ideal of goodness and new strength with which to realize it. This does not mean sudden transformation of the world, nor yet withdrawal from it to a detached plane of existence. It means that salvation takes place within the reality of people and things. The result is a very intricate situation, perhaps most clearly expressed in the teachings of the Apostle Paul on the relation between the old and the new man.

Thus salvation is hard to talk about, the more so since it is necessary, while keeping strictly to the statements of Revelation itself, to try to say something about perfect holiness, in other words, about the "motives" of God. Moreover, a practical consideration comes into the picture, and here I beg permission to speak personally. As in my previous book, *The End of the Modern World*, I should like to contribute to a subject which is of vital concern to everyone, and I am concerned lest the thoughts of this chapter might limit the circle of those to whom I address myself. On the other hand, it is obvious that our present situation demands clarity, so it must be to the good when in this day of watered-down theories and cure-all programs, the meaning of the Christian message is stated clearly and without compromise.

Let us get to the decisive point at once: namely, the person and attitude of Christ.

The sages of all great cultures were aware of the dangers of power and taught the means of overcoming them. Their most exalted doctrine on the subject is that of moderation and justice. Power seduces to pride and disregard for the rights of others. Hence over and against the tyrant is dangled the ideal of the man who remains considerate, who respects God and man, who defends justice. All this, however, is not salvation. It is an attempt to erect a stand, an order within disordered existence. It does not—as salvation must—embrace existence as a whole.[5]

From the viewpoint of our discussion, what is the decisive characteristic of the Christian message of salvation? It is expressed in a word which in the course of the modern age has lost its meaning: humility.[6]

Humility has become synonymous with weakness and paltriness, cowardice in a man's demands on existence, low-mindedness—briefly, the epitome of all that Nietzsche calls "decadence" and "slave morality." Such conceptions are innocent of the last trace of the phenomenon's real meaning. It must be admitted that in almost two thousand years of Christian history concepts of humility and forms of practicing it may be found which fit Nietzsche's description; but these are themselves signs of decadence, forms of decline from a greatness no longer understood.

True Christian humility is a virtue of strength, not of weakness. In the original sense of the word, it is the strong, high-minded, and bold, who dare to be humble. He who first realized the attitude of humility, making it possible for man, was God himself. The act by which this took place was the Incarnation of the Logos. St. Paul says in his letter to the Philippians that Christ "...being in the form of God, thought it not robbery [i.e., something which one does not possess by right and thus, out of weakness, clings to with anxiety] to be equal with God: But emptied himself, taking the form of a servant, being made in the likeness of men, and in habit formed as a man. He humbled himself, becoming obedient unto death, even to the death of the cross." (Philippians ii, 6-8)[7]

All creaturely humility has its origin in the act in which the Son of God became man. He accomplished it out of no personal need whatsoever, but out of pure freedom, because he, the Sovereign, willed it. The name of this "because" is Love. And it should be observed that the norm of Love is not to be found in what man has to say about it, but in what God himself says. For Love, like humility, as the New Testament points out, begins with God. (I John iv, 8-10)

How it is possible that he, the Absolute and Sovereign, can enter into existential unity with a human being; that he not only rules history but enters into it, taking upon himself all that such participation involves, namely "fate," in the true sense of the word—is beyond human comprehension. The moment we attempt to approach the mystery from mere natural philosophy, that is to say, from the concept of absolute being, the message of the Incarnation becomes mythology—or nonsense. The very attempt is nonsensical, for it would turn the whole order of existence upside down. We cannot say: God is thus and so, therefore he cannot do this or that. We must say: God does this, and in so doing reveals who he is. It is humanly impossible to judge Revelation. All we can do is to recognize it as a fact, and accept it, and judge the world and man from its standpoint. This then, is the basic fact of Christianity: God himself enters the world. But how?

The passage in the letter to the Philippians tells us: in the form of humility.

Consider Jesus' situation on earth: the way his mission progresses, molding his fate; his relations with people; the spirit of his acts, words, behavior. What you see over and over again is supreme power converted into humility. Just a few examples. By blood, Jesus descends from the old royal line, but it has declined and become insignificant. His economic and social conditions are as modest as possible. Never, not even at the peak of his activity, does he belong to any of the ruling groups. Of the men he selects for his associates, not one impresses us as personally extraordinary or particularly capable. After a brief period of activity, he is drawn into a sham trial. The Roman judge, partly bored, partly intimidated by the accusers, fails to uphold justice and sentences him to a death as dishonorable as it is agonizing.

It has been remarked, and rightfully, that the fate of the great figures of antiquity, even when it led to tragic downfall, always kept within a certain measure, within the set limits of what is permitted to happen to the great. In the case of Jesus, no such canon seems to exist; it seems that anything can happen to him. Isaiah's mysterious prophecy of the "slave of God" foreshadows this fate. (lii, 13, liii, 12)

In the same sense St. Paul speaks of *Kenosis*, the self-emptying act whereby he who was essentially in the *morphē theou*, the glory of god, gives himself into the *morphē tou doulou*, the lowliness of the slave.

Jesus' whole existence is a translation of power into humility. Or to state it actively: into obedience to the will of the Father as it expresses itself in the situation of each moment. And Jesus' situation, as a whole and in its parts, is one that demands constant self-renunciation. For the Son, obedience is nothing secondary or additional; it springs from the core of his being. Even his "hour" is shaped, not by his own will, but by his Father's. The paternal will becomes the filial; the Father's honor, Jesus' own honor. Not by succumbing to their demands, but in pure freedom.

Jesus' acceptance of "the form of a slave" signifies not weakness, but strength. The Gospels were written by simple men. They possess neither the epic scope of ancient historiography, nor the penetrating psychology to which we have become accustomed. Their narrative limits itself strictly to the immediate event and the evangelic word. Moreover, they are fragmentary, breaking off just when we desire to hear more. And they have other shortcomings which irritate the literary sensibility. An inmost attentiveness is needed to read them properly, but to him who achieves it, there unfolds an existence whose power is unique in history, a power that knows no outer bounds, only those self-imposed from within: the bounds of the Father's will accepted freely, and so completely accepted that at every moment, in every situation, deep into the heart's initial impulse, that will's demands are effective. It is strength that obeys here, not weakness. It is *kyriotes*, lordship, giving itself into slavery. Power so perfectly controlled that it is capable of renouncing itself utterly—in a loneliness as boundless as its dominion.

Once this much is clear, let us check backward and see whether among the great figures of history, there is any as great or even greater than Jesus, the Christ. Sometimes it appears so, but only as long as we take social or political efficacy, intellectual culture, spiritual profundity as our norms of greatness. When we touch the heart of the problem—and even to be aware of it requires the "eyesight" known as faith—the "superior qualities" of these great men reveal themselves for what they really are: talents and accomplishments within the world.

Jesus' existence, on the other hand, arches from the mystery of the living God, Sovereign over all that is "world," into present, concrete historicity. From such absolute superiority amidst the narrowest of historical bonds, he grasps the whole of creation, atones for its sin, and unseals the door to the new beginning.

Such is the New Testament's answer to the question of power. It does not condemn power as such. Jesus treats human power as the reality it is. He also knows what it is like; otherwise an event like the third temptation in the desert—which was temptation to *hybris*, pride—would make no sense (Matthew iv, 8-9). Equally evident, however, is the danger of power: the danger of revolt against God—the danger, above all, of no longer being aware of Him as the serious reality; the danger of losing the measure of things and lapsing into the arbitrary exercise of authority. To forestall this danger, Christ sets up humility, the liberator which breaks asunder the spell of power.

Yet for all of that, one might ask, what effect has Christ had upon history? Has the destructiveness of power been overcome through him? It is not an easy question to answer.

Salvation does not mean that the arrangements of the world have been changed once and for all, but that a new beginning of existence has been set—by

God. This beginning remains as a permanent possibility. Once and forever, God's attitude toward power is revealed; once and forever, through Christ's obedience, God's answer to the question of power is given—not privately, but publicly, historically, visible to all. It is not simply the isolated experience and victory of one individual that is here revealed, but rather an attitude in which all who will may share. And here the word "will" is to be understood in the full sense of the New Testament, embracing both the grace to be able to will and the decision of the will to act.

This beginning is there and can never be eradicated. How far its possibilities are realized is the business of each individual and each age. History starts anew with every man, and in every human life, with every hour. Thus at any moment it is free to begin again from the beginning thus established.

As for a concrete solution to our mortally grave problem of how to control power effectively, the answer—inasmuch as an answer is possible at all—must wait a little longer.

NOTES

1. Another symptom of that inner untruth of the contemporary attitude which we discussed in section one, *The End of the Modern World.*

2. Translator's note: One beautiful expression of this is the heraldic motto of the English kings, "I serve."

3. From this mythical ambiguity springs inordinate, covetous desire—just as, conversely, mythical deception is possible only when covetousness has made spiritual room for it. It is all a complex in which the various elements

alternately determine and "justify" one another, a vicious circle of wrong existence, chosen by man at the impenetrable beginning of his freedom. Genuine existence is determined spirally: purity of heart renders man more "seeing" for the truth; the truth perceived clears the way to deeper purity; deeper purity leads to higher knowledge; and so forth.

4. There are no myths of archetypal man. The now fashionable mytho-religiosity we meet on all fronts—historical, philosophical, aesthetic, psychological, political—is based on the totally unproven premise that man as he speaks to us in the myth is "natural" man. From this error stems the modern concept of the myth as a primal revelation of the meaning of existence. This premise is so dogmatic that contradiction is considered outright desecration. In reality, the myth is the self-expression of man *after* his first great test and its outcome. What speaks to us through the myth is not primal existence, but historical, in other words, fallen existence. And, again, not existence which had to fall in order to become historical, but existence which fell because man chose as he did. He could have chosen differently. All else is "tragicism" in which guilt tries to justify itself by insisting on its tragic "necessity." The Biblical is the only premise on which the myth—then, however, with profoundest implications—can be understood. (This whole question is one I hope to develop in detail in a special study.)

5. Buddhism seems to. But aside from the fact that there too the curve of the saving act never breaks out of the world, the radical means employed against the dangers of power consist in defining not only power, but all existence as meaningless. Salvation there would be the step into Nirvana.

6. How ill-prepared modern man is to form an opinion on humility, what a complete inner transformation he requires even to catch a glimpse of the phenomenon, we gather from Max Scheler's essay *"Zur Rehabilitierung der Tugend,"Abhandlungen und Aufsätze* (1915), Vol. I, pp. 3ff., esp. 8ff. (In later editions the essay appears under the title *"Vom Umsturz der Werte."*)

7. Douai version of the Holy Bible.

CHAPTER SIX

THE UNFOLDING OF POWER

[I]

Let us now try to draw a picture of the kind and extent of power which man has attained. Naturally we can attempt only the roughest sketch; to do this in detail would require no less than a history of culture.

Of primary importance are the earliest discoveries and means with which man confronted nature, a nature alien to him both intellectually and practically.[1] To these belong the first tools, such as knife, hammer, dipper, wheel, plough; the first weapons, club, spear, sling; the first protective raiment made possible by the tanning and joining of hides; weaving; the first remedies, fats and herbs. Also the elements of architectural construction, roof, support, door, steps; the first means of transportation, boat and roller; further, the planting of crops and domesticating of wild animals.

Not to be overlooked are the equally early artifacts which served no immediately practical purpose, though here we must remind ourselves that "purpose" (or "use"), as we understand the word, is a recent concept that cannot properly be applied to primitive life, in which everything, from garment to weapon, from plough to threshold, apart from its function—or rather, along with, in, and perhaps even preliminary to it—had symbolical-magical significance. Hence "purpose" is to be used here with utmost discretion. I have in mind things which for us would serve no practical purpose whatsoever: the various kinds of amulets to protect against malevolent spirits and insure the aid of benevolent—cult images, wall paintings, and so forth.

These early objects express something already in man entirely different from whatever it is that causes, for instance, a bird to build a nest. At first glance, it might seem that man is engaged in a similar process— that is, supplementing his bodily functions with certain objects which intensify those functions. In reality, right from the start, there is something in man which does not exist in the animal: man is aware—who can say how?—of the relation between cause and effect. He senses, even though he may not understand, the significance *behind* the forms and patterns of life, and he directs each aspect toward the realization of that meaning. In other words, his spirit is at work. Man rises above his natural surroundings. He surveys them, makes decisions, acts. He collects and develops experiences, takes them over from other men, and continues them.

A more painstaking study of prehistory would lead to the elemental processes of cultural creativity.

To understand these better, let us imagine a person

with extraordinarily alert instincts, keen and well-developed senses, lively play of the body as a whole and in its parts. As soon as the need for food or for relief from pain or for protection from danger becomes acute, he seeks it in his immediate surroundings or nearby. His instinct distinguishes between useful and harmful plants; his senses remark how a stone or piece of wood could increase his limbs' effectiveness; how matted branches or a hollowed log could help him to utilize a stream or the currents of lake or sea. Practical application proves, disproves, corrects the instinctive act, which in turn leads to fresh possibilities. In all this, the basic process is to be understood not merely as the discovery of a practical solution to a specific need, but rather as a series of relationships in which, step by step, one element determines the next. The curve of necessity as the ageless "mother of invention" goes full circle: the presence of the remedy also determining the nature and measure of the need. The process is based less on rational considerations than on acts of the instinct, of the creative and functional senses in whose play the interrelation of the whole becomes evident. A particularly important aspect is memory, one form of which is tradition. The power of early man to preserve and develop experiences is remarkably strong, both in the individual and in the community.

Other aspects of primitive man seem to have existed which are largely lost to civilized man today: awareness of things and events beyond his immediate ken; intuitions of forewarning and guidance supported by a subconscious not yet confused by reflection and reinforced by highly organized senses.

Primitive man experiences the whole of existence as something governed by mysterious forces. Everything rare and important in nature, things as well as processes, have a significance that extends far beyond the merely empirical. They are revelations of divine power, hence to be protected and hallowed. Even artifacts have such significance: house, fire, tool, weapon, ornament, vehicle, and so forth. The art of making them has been taught by higher beings, who also permeate and guard them. Thus the preservative forces we mentioned are essentially strengthened. Inventions are not forgotten and lost, but gathered into a lasting attention. The process of cultivation and endeavor never stops. From the treasury of collective achievements one possibility after the other is drawn; what has already been accomplished helps solve the problems to come.

All these forms of accomplishment are power, and their exercise constitutes mastery, sovereignty. The continuity of cultural creativity is thus established. Nature's raw materials and energies are discovered and utilized. As man's own natural abilities are organized in meaningful fashion, they are reinforced and their effectiveness as experienced in family and clan are comprehended, arranged, and developed into the various forms of social order.

[II]

This development progresses at a more or less steady pace from the earliest prehistoric epochs to the beginning of the modern age.

Indicative of the character of this whole period is the impression which the various cultures as well as the leaders of each age make upon us: their richest cultural creations bear an unmistakably human stamp. To indicate their rank in the history of human achievement we need only to name them: Athens' Acropolis, Peking's Forbidden City, the Cathedral of Chartres are peaks which later ages will not surpass, beside which they can only pose their own soaring accomplishments. But the old monuments seem to have been tempered by a moderation that is seldom violated (as it is, for instance, by certain Assyrian and occasional Roman constructions). Everything in man's world—his surroundings, achievements, works—are experienced as an immediate continuation and enhancement of his own being. It is to this impression of proportion and fittingness that the word "organic," currently much used to characterize the great cultures of the past, refers. The word (to be used with the necessary reservations) suggests that in ancient man's manner of interpreting nature, of reacting to it, utilizing and developing it, his rational, instinctive, and creative aspects held each other in check. He took possession of the given conditions, strengthened their forms, increased their effectiveness;

but on the whole, he respected their structure and did not break it up.[2]

Then something new happened. Man began to explore nature with methodical thoroughness and precision. It was no longer enough to comprehend it with his senses or to grasp it symbolically or practically. (We really ought to say that he gradually unlearned these approaches to nature.) Now he begins to disintegrate nature both experimentally and theoretically. He masters her laws and the requirements for making primary conditions produce direct, specific results. Thus functional relationships come into being that become progressively independent of direct human participation, relationships to which goals may be prescribed with even greater ease: technology.

Science as the rational comprehension of reality, and technology as the summary of scientific possibility, together stamp existence with a new mark: power or dominion in what might be called the "acute" sense of the word.

Nature is becoming more and more disintegrated, its energies ever more perfectly isolated; through increasingly precise mathematical-experimental methods, man bends nature to his will.

The machine is swiftly coming into its own. The tool increases the natural effectiveness of human limbs and organs; early forms of the machine were hardly distinguishable from tools. But the machine's development has been away from the implement towards something of its own that is quite different—

namely, a scientifically calculated and precisely constructed functional system that is growing increasingly independent of the human body. In its absolute form, the machine would be self-operating, self-regulating, and would automatically correct any possible malfunctioning caused by damage. Machines are being constructed today which actually approximate this ideal—how closely, we had better not try to say.

Individual machines are linked together, the one presupposing and continuing the product of the other, and the result is a factory. Various factories, technically and economically integrated, compose a production system. Now overall planning is unifying the production of entire countries.[3]

From all this a structural order evolves which has been invented and created by man, but which in its construction as well as in its effects is ever farther removed from direct human manipulation. It complies to human will and achieves human goals, but in the process it seems to develop a peculiar autonomy of function and growth.

This transformation of process and product is accompanied by a corresponding change in the working man himself. The handicrafts, on which all preceding culture was based, are disappearing. As the machine is perfected, the intimate relation of man to his work, in which his eye, hand, will, sense of material, imagination, and general creativeness cooperate, disappears. Process and product alike become ever farther removed from intellectual-physical norms and forces. They are founded on scientific knowledge and the practicalities of construction, and effected by mechanical processes.

As a result, in some respects, man himself grows poorer. He loses the rich satisfaction of personal creativity, consenting instead to invent, utilize, and service mechanical contraptions. But even as he puts them to ever more varied tasks, gaining through them ever greater power, his own will and creativeness must conform ever more to the mechanism in question, for one-sided effects do not exist. This means that the producer renounces individuality in his product and learns to content himself with producing only what the machine allows. The more perfect the apparatus, the fewer the possibilities for personal creativeness. And along with diminishing creativity, the human element, which lives so strongly in work made by hand, is also lost. In place of the artisan we have the worker, servicer of machines. For the customer too, something is lost, the personal contact with things that is possible only between persons and personally created objects. The customer is reduced to the modern consumer whose tastes are dictated by mass production, advertising, and sales techniques. And this to the point where he comes to consider the standards and values which only genuine craftsmanship can satisfy as senseless or effete.

On the other side of the balance-sheet, the achievements of science and technology pile steadily higher; the outlines of a gigantic total conception are beginning to be discernible, accompanied by the unleashing of corresponding, hitherto restricted, possibilities in man himself.

If nature is being more and more subjected to the control of man and his works, man himself is also increasingly controlled by those who fit him into "the system," even as his work is controlled by the end to which it is directed. Moreover, the consumer—in other words, everyone—now lives in a world of consumer goods, and hence in turn is constantly subjected to their influence.[4]

Indeed the consequences reach still farther. The culture which preceded technology's full break-through was characterized by the fact that man could experience personally what he theoretically perceived and physically created. Knowledge and creative possibility on the one hand, personal experience on the other, tallied in a measure which determined his whole attitude. From this blossomed that strikingly organic harmony so typical of pretechnical culture. Today the possibilities of knowing and doing progressively outstrip those of experiencing. The result is a world of thought, action, and works that are no longer capable of being experienced—a world that man has come to consider as an objective process complete in itself.

In the book cited at the beginning of this study, I suggested the term "non-human humanity" to describe the kind of human beings that are both the condition and the result of this process. Here I can only repeat: I know how misleading the expression is, but I am unable to find one better. It does not mean the inhuman being who, as a glance at history will prove, was possible also in the "human" epoch. It means man in whom the earlier relative agreement between the fields of knowledge and works on the one hand, and of experience on the other, is no longer found. He exists in a world of knowledge-works possibilities that have outstripped the earlier norms.[5]

Closely related to this, its cause and its result, is one of the most universal and most disturbing symptoms of the shift in the human condition that we have: the matter-of-factness of the new man.

In a way, this matter-of-factness demonstrates modern man's will and ability to concentrate on the task at hand regardless of personal feelings, to tasks that are becoming increasingly great and demanding; it demonstrates further his unwillingness, standing as he does ever more plainly in the public eye, to display emotions of any kind, indeed, even to harbor them. But it also evinces a growing inability to see, a progressive cooling of the heart, an indifference to the people and things of existence. A common substitute for genuine feeling is sensation, that superficial Ersatz-emotion—excitement, which, though momentarily strong, is neither fruitful nor lasting.[6]

Before going any further, we should pause for a consideration that will help us to bridge the first half of this study with the second. What has been said so far, could be interpreted as a description of humanity's decline. A large segment of current opinion actually does so interpret the historical process now unfolding. I beg to disagree.

The person who takes this stand, usually unconsciously of course, identifies the universally human with the humanity of a particular, though long, historical period. The number and variety of its phenomena mislead him; still more the fact that his own cultural roots are nourished by it. Thus he is prone to certain false conclusions. For one thing, he overlooks the negative possibilities that existed also in the past. Not without reason did we consider the theological aspects of power before the philosophical. Man's inner confusion as described by Revelation is characteristic, not of any one epoch but of all. It is part of fallen mankind. Naturally, from a Christian point of view, it is decline when the modern age as a whole draws away from Revelation; and it is understandable that the Christian interpretation of history dwells affectionately on the Middle Ages. However, it should not be forgotten that direct application of the truths of Revelation to world problems also has its dark side. The fact is too readily overlooked that Christian truths are by no means self-evident and that they speak of judgment as well as grace. Hence both their correct interpretation and their practical application presuppose a constant *metanoia* or conversion. Where this is absent, we have a pseudo-Christianity which leaves life's real substance untouched.

Considered thus, the pretechnical epochs also embraced all the possibilities of injustice and destruction—only these operated within a psychological climate whose basic organic harmony made them appear less harmful than they would be later. Seen in this larger view, the dangers which began to be evident in the modern age, and which are becoming ever more pressing, are but the revelation of possibilities which have existed in all ages.

To touch bottom, when we set up "the human" as a norm, what do we mean? We can mean the essence of all possibilities that exist in man: his various attitudes to the world, the tasks he faces, and the achievements which are his response to them. But people who feel more at home in the past than in the present are inclined to limit these many human possibilities to those which dominated history up to a certain point, be it the end of the Middle Ages, the beginning of modern times, the close of the early Victorian era, or the outbreak of World War I. Moreover, they are prone to consider the norms of their favorite epoch the sole guarantors of a sound, dignified human existence. Thus later developments are necessarily regarded as a decline from the essentially human— especially in certain circles devoted to an humanistic point of view.

But whenever this happens, the concept "man" is being conceived far too narrowly. For an essentially human characteristic is man's ability to cross the bounds of the organic-harmonious without becoming less "human" than he was before. Naturally, at such times the dangers we described come to the fore more strongly, more unambiguously than ever, so that, historically speaking, man does face the real and apparent crisis of his humanity. But "crisis" always means choice between positive and negative possibilities, and the real question is which way man's decision is to fall. If in the present crisis the dangers of the negative choice of injustice and destruction seem greater than ever before, only the intensity of those dangers is new, nothing essential, for these have always existed in man, not exclusively in the man of the future. All we can do is accept the present situation and, strengthened by the purest powers of the mind and of grace, overcome them from within. Should we fail, it would not be because our epoch as such is declining and falling; in all epochs man is in a state of decline and fall and in need of redemption—only in certain periods, under certain conditions, this fact can be concealed more easily than in others.

The above certainly does not mean that we should simply assent to whatever occurs today and will occur tomorrow. It is only a protest against the practice of identifying humanity at the decline of a particular period with humanity as such, and of laying the possibilities of destruction, so glaringly evident today, solely at the feet of the new epoch. That would be the kind of pessimism that insures defeat from the start.

But to return to our subject. The dissolution of organic creativity finds a counterpart in the dissolution of the basic unit of mature human life. The family is losing its significance as an integrating, order-preserving factor. Congregation, city, country are being influenced less and less by the family, clan, workgroup, class. Humanity itself appears ever more as a formless mass to be purposefully "organized."

This is of course conditioned by the population, which, compared to that of earlier ages, has increased disproportionately. The increase has been brought about by science and technology: natural catastrophes are more readily diverted; epidemics are quickly stamped out; hygiene, labor organizations, and social welfare agencies create better living and working conditions. However, the increase in population seems to be directly related to a decrease in man's originality. As population mounts, people grow more uniform, and families with genuine tradition and distinction become rarer, the possibilities of leading an individual life get fewer all the time. Modern cities everywhere are alike, whether in Western Europe, China, North or South America, or Russia. A type of man is evolving who lives only in the present, who is "replaceable" to a terrifying degree, and who all too easily falls victim to power.

The modern state shares the characteristics just described. It too is losing its organic structure, becoming more and more a complex of all-controlling functions. In it the human being steps back, the apparatus forward. Constantly improved techniques of stock-taking, man-power survey, and bureaucratic management—to put it brutally, increasingly effective social engineering—tend to treat people much as the machine treats the raw materials fed into it. From the standpoint of the bureaucracy in charge, any resistance on the part of those mistreated is equivalent to revolt, which must be crushed with ever more refined techniques and greater stringency.

As for the peoples of the world, for the time being they continue to be those vast bodies of human beings determined by geography, race, culture, who are becoming capable of history within a national framework. But whereas formerly these ethnic groups showed unmistakable individuality, today they are growing more and more alike. Their mutual economic and political dependence grows constantly greater, their dress and way of life more similar. The nations' political structure and methods of operation are largely interchangeable. This equalizing of ethnic and political individualities seems to contradict the phenomenon of modern nationalism, which has developed in sharp contrast to the unity of the medieval West. That unity, however, was built by spirit and faith, and it left the lives and cultures of the various races their freedom, whereas the levelling process of the modern age springs from the rationality of science and functionalism of technology. Perhaps modern nationalism is the peoples' last attempt to defend themselves against absorption—a defense by means of a formal system which will, however, gradually succumb to other still more abstract principles of power.

When we examine the development as a whole, we cannot escape the impression that nature as well as man himself is becoming ever more vulnerable to the domination—economic, technical, political, organizational—of power. Ever more distinctly our condition reveals itself as one in which man progressively controls nature, yes, but also men; the state controls the citizens; and an autonomous technical-economic-political system holds all life in thrall.

This growing defenselessness against the inroads of power is furthered by the fact that ethical norms have lost much of their influence, hence their ability to curb abuses of power is weakened.

Ethical norms are valid by their own inner truth, but they become historically effective by taking root in man's vital instincts, inclinations of the soul, social structures, cultural forms and traditions. The process we have been studying breaks these ancient rootholds. They are replaced—at least temporarily—by formalistic rules and regulations and by the various techniques known as "organization." But organization does not create an ethic.

Thus the importance of ethical norms in men's lives gives way to stress on mere expediency. This is true above all of those norms which protect the person. Just one example. Not very long ago, it was considered a sacrilege to dissect a corpse—not, as self-glorifying modernity insists, because the Middle Ages were backward, but because men still harbored an instinctive reverence for the human body, even when dead. From this we can measure the terrible speed with which one bulwark of reticence after the other has been torn down. For the average sentiment, does anything at all remain that is still untouchable? Are not experiments on living bodies being performed constantly? Were the practices in certain "scientifically-minded" concentration camps any different from vivisection? Trace the connecting line which leads from control of human conception to interrupted pregnancy; from artificial insemination to euthanasia; from race-breeding to the destruction of undesirable life. What may one *not* do to people if by "one" we mean the average man we encounter everywhere, in the street, in our newspapers, on the screen, radio and television, in literature and drama, and, most ominous of all, in our statesmen, lawmakers, military and economic leaders?

When man drops the ethical reins, he places himself utterly at the mercy of power. Never could he have sunk as low as he did in Germany's all-too-recent past, never could he suffer such abuse as he continues to suffer right now in other parts of the world, had he not been so abandoned by his ethical sense and his feeling for his own personal being. As we have pointed out more than once, a one-sided causality simply does not exist among living things. One being affects another as much as that other allows himself to be affected, indeed, cooperates in the process. In the long run, domination requires not only the passive consent, but also the will to be dominated, a will eager to drop personal responsibility and personal effort. Broadly speaking, the dominated get what they themselves desire; the inner barriers of self-respect and self-defense must fall before power can really violate.

A further point: life's religious content is steadily disintegrating. This does not necessarily mean that Christian faith is losing its influence on general conditions (though naturally this too can be true) but something more elemental for man—namely, that the direct religious valuableness of existence is escaping him.

In primitive cultures, everything is religiously determined. Everything significant in man's life and work has a religious root which warrants its existence. The measurements with which he measures; the media he uses for exchange; tool and weapon, threshold and field-marker; the location of a city and its form, determined by the market-place at its heart and the walls which enclose it; natural objects, each with its special significance for man; the animals he hunts—all come from the divine and possess mysterious powers. As critical thought takes over, as man becomes lord of nature, as various natural spheres are abstracted from the original whole, man's awareness of these powers declines.[7]

Modern man cuts himself off not only from the community and from tradition, but also from his religious connections. He is indifferent both to the specific, once-authoritative Christian Credo, and to religious ideas in general. Things, forces, processes have become "worldly"—the word stripped of its former religious richness and given a new sense which implies "rationally understandable and technically controllable." This means that both man as a whole as well as important individual aspects of human life—the defenselessness of childhood, the special nature of woman, the simultaneous physical weakness and rich experience of the aged—all lose their metaphysical worth. Birth is now considered merely the appearance of a new unit of the species *homo sapiens;* marriage but an alliance of a man and a woman with certain personal and legal consequences; death the end of a total process known as life. Happiness or unhappiness are no longer providential, but simply lucky or unlucky accidents with which a man must cope as best he can. Things lose their mystery, transparency, becoming calculable forms with specific economic, hygienic, aesthetic values. History no longer bears any relation to a Providence emanating wisdom and benevolence, it is a mere string of empirical processes. The majesty of the state no longer reflects divine majesty; it exists not "by the grace of God," but solely by grace of the people. Or to put it less irreverently and more sensibly, the state is the organizational apparatus of the people and operates according to psychological, sociological laws. It becomes progressively independent of the people, whom it ultimately dominates completely. All this strengthens and seals the process we described: man, with all he is and has, places himself ever more unreservedly at the disposal of power.

This process leads straight to a concept whose consequences cannot be overestimated: the idea of universal planning. Under such planning man would control everything before him—not only raw materials and natural energies, but also living man in his entirety. Statistics would make an exact inventory of the material at hand. Theory would demonstrate the means of utilizing it. "National interest" would determine the general goal. Technology would provide the methods with which to attain it.

Universal planning is being prepared with weighty arguments: political necessity, increased population, limited resources and the need for better distribution, the magnitude of modern technical problems, and so forth. But the real drives behind it are spiritual rather than practical; they culminate in an attitude which feels it to be its right and duty to impose its own goal upon mankind—and to utilize all that is as material for the realization of its earthly "kingdom."

NOTES

1. The word "alien" has connotations of varying depths. For one, it suggests merely that early man did not comprehend nature and control it. Underlying this conception, and knowable only through Revelation, is a profounder one, namely, alienation as the result of guilt. In other words, man confronts nature with claims that contradict his creaturely essence, with the result that nature obstructs and resists him. Much could be said on this point. Careful analysis of the man-nature relation would unearth basic cultural facts conducive to a new realism and quite a different level of profundity from those of the usual naturalistic-idealistic interpretations.

2. These statements are, of course, only rough approximations. In earlier epochs, too, forms and attitudes existed which destroyed the balance of things. Whenever this happened, civilization became a groundless, precariously hovering thing, whose peril the mythical figure of Icarus perfectly expresses. Nevertheless, for the ancient cultures as a whole, the impression of organic harmony is inescapable, and it grows stronger as we look back upon it from ever more "modern" circumstances.

3. Consider the systematic unifying of German industrial norms and the geographical unification of the Tennessee Valley. Translator's note: also the industrial program of the Common Market countries.

4. Translator's note: Compare Galbraith's *The Affluent Society*.

5. Let us take an example. If a man attacks and kills another with a club,

he experiences his act directly. It is quite another thing when he pulls a lever in an airplane at high altitude, and hundreds of thousands perish in cities far below him. He is capable of knowing and of causing such an act; he is no longer capable of experiencing it as act and event. In various ways this is true also for much else in contemporary life.

6. Sensation has found perfect organs of expression in the press, cinema, radio, and television. It is so much at home, so firmly entrenched in these media, that in moments of real perception we are bound to shudder.

7. Christianity also contributed to the breaking of the immediate religious hold of existence. Its richness had overwhelmed man, making the world itself seem divine and rendering man its prisoner. Revelation's tidings of a sovereign God, who created the world and who will come to judge it, broke open the dungeon. In the process, natural religion's ardent experience of being, a matter of temperament and religious historical development, was not annulled; it continues to be effective—only now it is purified by the God of Revelation, regulated and channelled into the various forms of tradition and cult. Yet clearly the process was one of disenchantment. Thus in his immediate religious response to the world the Christian, like the Old Testament believer before him, was much less "pious" than the one-time heathen. Here is the clue to the heathen state's paradoxical indictment of Christians for their "godlessness." Under quite different circumstances, similar accusations against the Church have been made repeatedly by the national states which came into being after the Reformation—charges of "enmity toward the state." Their most recent version comes from the modern totalitarian state, which insists that every believer as such is an instrument of "sabotage." It would be rewarding to trace the burden of this theme with its variations, from Jesus' mock-trial to the present day.

CHAPTER SEVEN

THE NEW CONCEPT OF THE

WORLD AND OF MAN

[I]

Where, ultimately, is it all leading?

The usual answer runs something like this: By means of ever more penetrating science and effective techniques, man's power over the world's given conditions steadily mounts. This means increased security, usefulness, well-being, progress. Human life and health will be better protected; people will work less; the living standard will improve; there will be new possibilities for personal and occupational development; man will accomplish greater things with less effort and enjoy an even richer life.

Taken separately, these claims are obviously true. It is an unquestionable gain when social tensions are more easily recognized and eased; when food distribution is better regulated; when distances can be covered faster. But what about the picture as a whole?

No one in his senses would question, for example, the importance of modern medical achievements. He has only to fall ill himself or care for a fellow sufferer to appreciate them. But in medicine, as in everything else, one aspect is related to another, and each to the whole. When we examine that whole—medical science, hygiene, therapeutic techniques, the pharmaceutical industry, health insurance and public health financing, not forgetting contemporary man's attitude, both as doctor and as patient, toward health and sickness—when we realize that this gigantic apparatus is directed at the individual, living person, affecting each one differently, so that each in turn must adjust himself to it—when we weigh all these aspects conscientiously, do we really come out ahead? Or do we discover, to mention just one point, that precisely that is endangered which, with due respect to exact knowledge and methods, still remains the foundation of all therapy, namely, man's will to health, his vital confidence, sure instinct, and natural powers of self-renewal?

Again: The advantages of a well-planned, dependable insurance system are indisputable. Sickness, unemployment, accidents, old age, and so on lose much of their terror when the material needs are assured. But let us imagine the goal of insurance-experts realized: one organization for all citizens, covering every possible need. What, in the long run, would be its effects upon the average man? What would become of personal conscientiousness and prudence, of independence and character, of healthy confidence and readiness for whatever comes? Wouldn't such a system of total, automatic welfare be also a system of tutelage? And, along with all that, wouldn't man's feeling of being led to his destiny by providence gradually disappear?

Or again: When traffic moves more swiftly, smoothly, will people really gain time? They would, if improved transportation meant more rest and leisure. But does it? Aren't people more rushed than ever? Don't they actually stuff more and more into the time they save by getting places faster? And when man does have more leisure, what does he do with it? Does he really break away from the pressures of life, or does he fling himself into more and more crowded pleasures, more exaggerated sports; into reading, hearing, and watching useless stuff; so that in reality, spirit-impoverishing busyness continues, only in other forms, and the beautiful theory of the richer life of leisure proves to be one more self-deception?

No matter where we start from, invariably we arrive at the same fundamental conclusion: the fundamental correction of cultural ills does not lie in the adoption of utilitarian reforms; however great their immediate advantages, their dangers are greater still. In the last analysis, the quality of culture is determined by the decisions of the spirit. And that means that man, as he has ever greater power at his disposal, leads a life of ever greater peril.

What is it, then, that inexorably drives us to seek power?

When we examine the motives of human endeavor and the play of forces set in motion by historical decisions, we discover everywhere a basic will at work, the will to dominion. Here lies the taproot of human greatness and tragedy, joy and sorrow. The ability to rule was made an essential, God-given part of man's nature at the time of his creation. The permission to rule is a privilege by divine consent. The obligation to rule is mission. Since the Fall, it is also man's fate and continuous, arduous test.

How, on the whole, does man rule? Through knowledge. He desires to know the world in order to give it a new face. This is the goal of culture, and the road to its fulfillment leads through mounting dangers.

Behind the attempts at world-renewal beckons an image by which man attempts to express the essence of things, of his own being, and of the meaning of life. The struggle for dominion is the struggle to realize that image.

It is always difficult to discuss things that are only just coming into existence, but perhaps a few features of the emerging world's new aspect are already recognizable. We described the world view of antiquity, classical man's attempt to express the self-contained harmony of a divinely conceived universe and the noble human being. The Middle Ages tried to order existence from a point of authority and holy power not in existence, but "above" it. Modernity tried by means of rationality and exact techniques to bring nature to heel. And our present, emergent view of the world? As power continues to increase, indeed, as it seems to attain a definite form (if, in view of history any form may be called definite) awareness of its dangers also increases, and more and more, man realizes that the crux of the coming existence will be the control of power itself.

[II]

First of all, let us try to get the dangers of power into focus.[1]

Man is learning to control both things and people ever more fully. But how? He is free to use power as he wills, a freedom determined by his own attitude. But what is contemporary man's attitude toward his responsibility?

In a recent analysis of our present situation, we find the following disturbing lines concerning "the crisis of our age and of our world": "...we seem to be rushing toward an event which from the human point of view can only be described as global catastrophe...between us and that event only a few decades remain. This respite is characterized by steadily growing technical possibilities that are directly proportionate to a decrease in man's awareness of his responsibility."

Obviously, such sweeping statements should be met with reserve. Nonetheless, we ought to test them. Do the men and women we know, each of us in his own field, strike us as people conscious of *their* responsibility for what is happening in the world? Does their sense of responsibility affect their public as well as their private lives? Do our rulers impress us as people who know what their duties ultimately involve and who tackle them accordingly? Is every public servant's measure of power counterbalanced by strength of character, adequate understanding of human existence, and a fitting moral attitude? Has an ethic of power evolved from a real coming to grips with the phenomenon of power? Are young people (and older ones too as far as possible) being educated to the right use of power? Does such education form a substantial part of both of our individual and our public endeavors?

I fear that honest answers to these questions would be most disquieting. We cannot escape the impression that the public is ignorant of what it is all about, and that most of those who do know are completely at sea as to what should be done, so they let things drift.

Let us try to pinpoint the dangers.

First and most obvious is the danger of violent destruction. There still seem to be people who set their hopes on war. The destruction of human life and talents, of economic and cultural goods which a new war would involve, surpasses understanding.[2] Greater still would be the spiritual losses. The last remnants of spiritual-ethical order, of respect for man, of character and inner security, would crumble. The result would be a long-lived attitude of belief solely in violence and trickery: nihilism fulfilled. And this would apply also to the victors—inasmuch as the term, a hangover from a passing order of things, still has any meaning, and we are not forced to speak, as indeed we already have been, of mere survivors. Any future war would be universal and would involve all mankind.[3]

Not so directly tangible, but looming on all sides

is another danger. Man is acquiring ever more power over man, an ever profounder influence over him physically, intellectually, spiritually; but how will he direct that influence?

One of the most terrible lessons which those whose cultural roots reach back before World War I had to learn, was that in concrete existence the spirit is much weaker than they had supposed. They were convinced that its influence was direct, hence that it must inevitably triumph over violence and cunning. "The human spirit cannot be suppressed for long." "Truth will prevail." "The real values will win in the end." At the very least, this idealistic notion of the spirit's immediacy and protective faculties was false. Those who entertained it had to learn the painful way how far the power of the state with its public-conditioning organs reaches, and to what terrifying degree it is possible to cripple the spirit, cow the individual, confuse the norms of the valid and the just.

Instead of "everything coming out all right," what actually happened? Which value that modernity believed itself so secure in (in proud comparison with the "dark" Middle Ages) was not denied? Which of all culture's achievements remained unscathed? The dignity of truth and the loftiness of justice; human dignity; the inviolability of man's spiritual and physical being; freedom of the individual, of personal enterprise; the right to private opinion; freedom of speech; the trustworthiness of public servants, not only in regard to the letter of their instructions, but also to the spirit behind them; the freedom of science, art, education, medicine each to be answerable to its own deepest purpose—which of these was not destroyed? Have not violence and deceit become established practice? And let us nurse no illusions: these things took place not only in the temporary confusion of anarchy, but within the studied pattern of theoretical and practical systems carefully prepared.

Can, then, the spirit sicken? Not only its physiological organs of brain and nervous system, not only on the psychological level of sense-activity, the imaginative processes, and so forth, but the spirit itself *qua* spirit? On what does its health depend? First Plato and later in the fullness of Revelation St. Augustine made this clear: the health of the spirit depends on its relation to truth, to the good and the holy. The spirit thrives on knowledge, justice, love, adoration—not allegorically, but literally. What happens when man's relation to these is destroyed? Then the spirit sickens. Not as soon as it errs or lies or is guilty of an injustice; it is difficult to say just how many such "exposures" to disease the spirit can withstand before it succumbs to that inner blindness, that destruction of all proficiency, which are the symptoms of spiritual decline. However, this much is certain: once truth as such loses its significance; once success usurps the place of justice and goodness; once the holy is no longer perceived or even missed, the spirit is stricken indeed. What then occurs is no longer a matter for psychology; then no therapeutical measures help; the only thing that can save is conversion, *metanoia*. Seen from this viewpoint, how heavily do they weigh, the twelve-year experiment in Germany and that almost four times as old in the East?

Yet one of these systems did last twelve years, and what brought it low came not from within but from without. The other has outlasted decades, growing mightily all the while. We dare not underrate the historical power of such experiments—still less, as the whole fabric of our present-day life, with its rationalization and mechanization, its techniques of forming public opinion, and its control of education, is a tempting preparation for outright imitation. It can be an effective temptation even when specifically accepted and expressed ideas apparently oppose it, for usually it is the enemy who dictates the methods, and methods are often stronger than ideas.

A third danger is the effect that naked power—*i.e.*, violence—has over existence. There are things which can well be controlled by rational power: everything connected with inanimate nature, for instance. As soon as we progress to animate nature, it is another story; intuition and sensitivity immediately become essential. And when we reach the human order—all that has to do with education, welfare, culture, civil services—we find ourselves on territory where everything, to remain human and be spiritually successful, must first pass through the "personal center," that inmost core of the responsible human heart. The true, the good, and the right are realizable only if accepted by living people with inner, genuine conviction, and to bring this about requires reverence, encouragement, patience. He who would be truly effective with men must respect *their* freedom, stir *their* initiatives, awaken *their* creative centers. Working with the impulses of living persons, he must freely accept all their false starts and detours.

The greater a man's power, the stronger the temptation to take the shortcut of force: the temptation to nullify the individual and his freedom, to ignore both his creative originality and his personal truth; to achieve the desired end simply by force, dismissing what cannot be forced as not worthy of consideration—in other words, the temptation to erect a culture on rational and technical foundations alone. To this end, man himself must be considered something "marketable" ("the labor market"), something that can be "managed"—*i.e.*, "laid off or on," "conditioned" from the start to certain ends.[4] Even spiritually man is malleable, once dialectics and mass-suggestion, propaganda and *Weltanschauung* or historical perspective, even legal testimony are undertaken not with respect for truth, but to support predetermined ends. Then the truly spiritual, that tension between the beholding, judging human being and that which he beholds, the valid, lies slack.

A fourth and final danger: that which power holds for those who wield it. Nothing corrupts purity of character and the lofty qualities of the soul more than power. To wield power that is neither determined by moral responsibility nor curbed by respect of person results in the destruction of all that is human in the wielder himself.

Antiquity was profoundly aware of this danger. It knew man's greatness, but also his vulnerability, so fatefully augmented by power. Only through moderation, by scrupulously maintaining his spiritual balance, could man preserve his existence. For Plato, the tyrant (*i.e.*, wielder of power), who was not held in check by reverence for the gods and respect for the law, was a forlorn and doomed figure. Little by little modernity lost this knowledge. Things that are now common practice—the denial of any norm higher than man, the public consent to autocratic power, the universal use of power for political or economic advantage—these are without precedent in history.

In this context, "wielder of power" does not mean only those responsible for our national and international political and economic policies, but anyone who possesses "power"—power to make important decisions, give orders, direct people, cause effects, create conditions—in Biblical terminology, anyone who exercises "dominion." Man's ability to do so likens him to the Lord of heaven and earth; here lie the roots of human greatness. But as we tried to point out in Chapter Five, in man the relation between power and its direction, between energy and measure, impulse and order are profoundly confused. Hence there is great danger of mistaking violence for power, self-glorification for initiative, subjection for authority, advantage for justice, and success for genuine, permanent effectiveness; and the danger increases as the curbs of ethical norms and religious awe are weakened.

Even more threatening is the perversion of power and the consequent perversion of human nature itself. For no effect is operative in one direction only, be it toward a thing or a person; always it influences its agent as well.

It is a dangerous illusion to think that a deed can remain "outside" the doer. In reality, it permeates him, is in him even before it reaches the object of his act. The doer is constantly becoming what he does—every doer, from the responsible head of state to office manager or housewife, from scholar to technician, artist to farmer. Hence if the use of power continues to develop as it has, what will happen to those who use it is unimaginable: an ethical dissolution and illness of the soul such as the world has never known.

[III]

In the process of upheaval and remolding which is taking place around us can we discover any elements that bear upon these dangers? Can we say that the structure of historical existence now building will be prepared to meet them?

Again I must insist: anything we say on this subject is necessarily mere conjecture, for everywhere things are still fluid, quite apart from the fact that interpretation of contemporary events is bound to be deeply colored by the personal attitude of their interpreter. All we really know is that where the destructive elements are so violent, historical conditions so precarious, and human attitudes so confused, grounds for pessimism are, to say the least, as solid as for optimism. My personal opinion must be clear from the foregoing. Nevertheless, I wish to repeat, expressly, that I believe in the possibility of a positive solution—not in the old, liberal sense of letting things "take care of themselves," still less in agreement with that historical-dialectical optimism which insists that all things necessarily move toward something better. Such attitudes only endanger the chances of a positive outcome, for they fail to alert those forces on which, ultimately, everything depends: the personal responsibility of free men. I am convinced that such freedom has a real chance to swing history into a happier direction.

An important fact in the new view of the world is its finiteness. To be sure, science and technology reckon with stupendous figures that both multiply and divide themselves past comprehension. Nonetheless, we have only to compare the dominant mood today with that at the dawn of the modern age to see the difference. Time and space, matter and energy reveal themselves in dimensions little dreamed of by modernity, yet we no longer conceive of them as infinite, as the preceding age with its incomparably narrower "given conditions" so passionately insisted.

For the modern age, "world" stood for the "all"— not only quantitatively, but qualitatively, since it was absolute and boundless. Thus man could never take a stand confronting the world, only one within it. The world overwhelmed him, literally and essentially.

He could neither really "distance" himself from it nor criticize it; for him the only possibility as part of it was to unite himself with it. Granted, this union of himself with the world gave him a sense of immeasurable fullness of being, of inexhaustible reserves; but it made any interchange, any "dialog" between himself and the world impossible.

The feeling that is beginning to permeate our own age is that the world is something shaped, hence limited. The measure of those limits is colossal in both directions, great and small, but they *are* measured. The term the "all" seems to be acquiring a new significance. No longer does it mean simply the reverence-demanding exaltedness of being as such, nor yet the call of infinite to dionysian surrender, but rather the sum-total of "the given," which not only permits man to take a stand, to judge the world, to plan for it, but also demands these things of him. Today it is much easier for man to experience himself as he really is: someone in the world, yet "outside" it; bound by its laws yet free to confront it; someone, so to speak, on the edge of the world, everywhere and forever on its frontiers.

This basic feeling begets a different attitude to the world. It is harsher, harder, yet it keeps man's head and hands peculiarly free. The world no longer overpowers; it challenges—a challenge that calls for intellectual-spiritual responsibility.

Something similar is beginning to reveal itself in that field of practical activity which is forced to reckon with the most important of earthly norms, the political—"politics" understood in its real meaning of activities of peoples and governments taken in definite areas at definite times. Modernity could bask in dreams of yet undiscovered lands, untapped reserves. The concept "colony" was an expression of this. Even the individual peoples and their states embraced, both materially and humanly speaking, unknown, unmeasured possibilities. Hence there was a certain justification for the light-hearted assumption that more substance existed than would be used, more energy than that recorded. Today the world has shrunk to a single political field with no gaps or empty spaces. On the international scene, what were once political objects are becoming, as we watch, political subjects: the phenomenon of the colony is vanishing like smoke. On the national, by means of statistical techniques and intensive administration, the living standards, goods, and energies of lands and peoples are known and controlled ever more completely.

As a result, political problems turn more and more from the extensive to the intensive. "Governing"—in the true sense of observing, judging, comprehending, directing, evaluating the given part in view of the whole—becomes particularly urgent. In this closed field every measure has a much sharper effect, for good or for evil. Its force is not dissipated in limitless surroundings, but rings out in closed space, a clear summons to responsibility which cannot pass unheard. Perhaps the pathological growth of bureaucracy presents not only a negative symptom of our times, but also a kernel of truth: historical-political conditions are far more malleable now than formerly and hence must be approached with greater awareness and precision than in the past. All the bumbling intricacy and crude attempts at leading people around displayed by modern bureaucracy may be reflections of the contemporary state's insufficient comprehension of this fact.

The growing, universal awareness of the world as a unit seems to be another pointer in the same direction. Instead of the earlier atomistic interpretation, according to which existence consisted basically of discrete entities grouped according to viewpoint, we have today an ever deeper realization that all existence rests on certain basic forms, and that the individual form is part of a whole, which in turn is affected by the individual. From this springs the awareness that everything affects everything. Those who remember with what dogmatic certainty end-of-the-century rationalism explained all events by a one-sided causality, dismissing the concept of a final cause as Scholastic humbug, are now amazed at the reappearance of that concept as something "new," and amused to see it applied so radically that we can speak of a reversal of causality, in other words, of a causation working backwards into the past.

Politically, in the broadest meaning of the word, we are approaching a state in which the economic, social, national conditions of one country have repercussions all over the world. Just as no one class in a country can long remain in poor social, economic, or hygienic conditions without affecting the whole nation, so also no particular group can flourish long and truly when conditions as a whole are not in good order.

Indeed, people are beginning to realize that the same sort of interdependence that exists between individuals and groups also holds true for religious and secular attitudes. In our own time we have seen modernity's insistence on the private nature of a man's *Weltanschauung* completely overturned. The dogmatic, all-encompassing control so popularly ascribed to the Middle Ages was sheer liberalism compared with that exercised by National Socialism and progressively developed and perfected by Communism. Let us for a moment disregard the violation of all truths and human dignity that was and is largely practiced by such systems—it is significant that they found they could not leave any aspect of existence out of account. What we call personal freedom, independence, self-possession must be quite different from what the old liberal attitude thought them to be; rather, the inner world in which a man lives with himself is intimately linked with the reality of existence. The view that religion is something purely subjective, and the opposite view that is to be determined by the state are so closely related that they may be regarded as two facets of the same fundamental error.

In the realm of immediate human values, present-day biology and medicine realize with growing clarity that the function of the individual organ affects the whole organism, and conversely, the condition of the whole is shared by each part. Hence there is no physical ailment that is not psychologically conditioned, just as every psychic-intellectual process presupposes specific physical conditions.

The broadest expression of this tendency in current thought may be found in the growing importance of the concept of relativity. By this I do not mean the disintegrating relativism of the foregoing epoch, which stripped given conditions of their own special worth, constantly referring each aspect back to the preceding one and so destroying the original phenomenon. If I understand it correctly, today's conception of relativity gives it a new and different significance. It attempts to show that being is always a totality, the various aspects of which exist with, through, and in relation to one another. This is seen in such elementary phenomena as the act of knowing, in which the object cannot be considered apart from the subject, in which the observer and the observed coinhere; or again, in regard to causality, in which there exist no one-sided effects among beings, but every effect is bipolar.

Thus here too we have the phenomenon of comprehensiveness in good as in evil. Hence what should be demanded of any proper governance or "rule" is that it be firmly grounded in knowledge of how the various energies of existence affect one another, and in a deep sense of responsibility for existence, whose many reciprocal effects render it especially vulnerable.

The modern world view conceived of a nature that was as much its own norm as it was a system of security. Nature was considered to be a complicated apparatus of laws and interrelations which on the one hand bound man, and on the other safeguarded and warranted his existence. Today, knowledge and technology are breaking up the natural forms. Even the elements are open to seizure. Once a sovereign and protective harmony, nature today is a mere sum of matter and energies under man's control. Once an inviolable, awe-and-joy-inspiring whole, nature is becoming an inexhaustible Possibility, Dynamo, Workshop. And whereas in the modern age man considered himself a part or a "member" of nature, the feeling today is that he can "handle" it in unlimited freedom, bending it to his will for prosperity or destruction.

Similar changes are affecting also the inherited patterns of existence and the various forms of tradition, which in the West were stamped by Christianity and Humanism, and in Asia and Africa by their own religious-cultural past. Once the individual participated fully in his tradition; he was both shaped and protected by it. Today tradition everywhere is disintegrating. Characteristically, novelty is now accepted as value *per se.* The desire to change everything seems to be more than a mere symptom of change in generations; more than the discoverer's eagerness to prove the importance of his discovery. Naturally enough, it has negative forms: irreverence, irresponsibility, sensationalism. But beneath these something positive seems to be at work: the feeling that to a degree hitherto undreamed the world lies at man's disposal, and that man's right use of the world is guaranteed neither by nature nor by tradition, but depends upon his personal insight and will.

We have already discussed at some length the element of danger that lies herein, so we need only remind ourselves of it once more. It does not belong exclusively to the negative symptoms of the coming culture. If it did, we could only conclude: then away with it! But danger is an integral part of the coming world view, and when rightly understood, it lends that view a new earnestness. To the end of time there will be no human existence that does not live with peril.

Awareness of this is lively, and not without the usual unworthy companions of fear, superficiality, the eat-drink-and-be-merry-*now* attitude we meet everywhere. But it has its positive symptoms too: the bourgeois devotion to security seems to be waning, and man is beginning to free himself from many involvements that formerly he took for granted. The fact that entire populations have been uprooted and transplanted, that the old conception of home is fast disappearing and an almost nomadic form of life taking its place, that people today have lost interest in savings accounts and are changing their attitude to the various types of insurance—all this and more suggests not only the negative aspect of general rootlessness, but also a positive: that in response to the unknown, unknowable dangers of the future, man is attempting to gain a larger measure of mobility. The feeling is growing that everything is an open question, because ultimately everything depends on freedom; therefore man himself must develop an attitude of greater freedom. What a curious development hard on the heels of classical natural science, according to which everything was determined by necessity, hence was insurable!

Lastly, characteristic of the nascent world are its markedly greater mobility, flexibility, potentialities, as compared with those of the world view which preceded it.[5]

This can be demonstrated from various angles. Let us take one. Until now the human body was considered a closed system which developed its own potentialities, acted on its own impulses, and regulated itself. Into this closed corporality the individual medical theoretician or practitioner whenever he deemed it necessary introduced the soul, spirit, leaving the question of its relation to the rest to be answered usually by some dualistic concept.

These views are changing radically. The present-day conception of the human body is of something not complete in itself, not clearly defined, not autonomous. It appears more like something in vital motion, almost an event that is continually happening—an event determined by the spirit. Or to put it more exactly, man seems to be something that realizes itself between two poles: the material and the psychic-spiritual.[6] Evidence of this is the increasingly effective insight of medical science into the psychosomatic nature of all bodily processes, particularly those directly related to illness and health. Pointing in the same direction is another concept, one which Nietzsche discusses at great length and even develops into a program: breeding, the idea that man's living substance may be influenced by appropriate measures. Whether or to what extent this is valid is an open question. What interests us here is that the theory indicates once again that the living human being is conceived as something much more mobile and with far greater potentialities than was supposed in the past. Consequently, he is also in far graver danger.

Once our attention has been called to this particular aspect of the new image of the world, we see it again and again. Everywhere things reveal themselves as far less "fixed," more fluid and more amenable to human initiative than the nineteenth century ever dreamed.

All we have said—and much more could be added—heightens the growing awareness of man's responsibility.

Complicated motives lay behind the modern world's concept of nature. Primarily, there was the will to be free for autonomous world dominion— from which, however, it would follow that self-glorious man should assume genuine responsibility for his actions. But for finite beings there is no such thing as autonomous responsibility; in claiming it, man usurps what belongs to God. Thus purely "human responsibility" is only seemingly fulfilled, and that only for as long as the echoes of the Christian tidings of divine creation and governance still reverberate. In reality, the notion already contains the concept which would consume the last vestiges of responsibility for the world—namely, the idea of nature as infinite and eternal, all in all, embracing even man. Once that idea was entertained, *via* whatever empirical or metaphysical detours man might choose, only one course remained open to him: to fit himself into the whole, with various rationalistic, evolutionary, sociological theories only providing this basic aim with more or less scientific underpinnings. Whereas real freedom is warranted only in view of a sovereign and personal God, and real responsibility is possible and binding only in relation to him, an omnipotent Nature would absorb freedom and responsibility alike. For all the mind's seeming independence, All-nature, not man, would determine history, hence also warrant it.

This concept is now revealing itself more and more clearly to be false. Man, not nature, determines things. And not from necessity, which would render him a kind of nature once-removed, but in freedom. Awareness of this is beginning to penetrate the most varied fields. One typical example is extreme existentialism, which swings back the pendulum from the former all-determination of nature to a radical freedom that is as unrealistic as the concept against which it is reacting. This version of reality consumes all of truth's substance, leaving man in pure arbitrariness; in other words, everything becomes meaningless.

There is no help for it; man can only go back—or ahead—to the truth in which the saving *metanoia* may be realized. He cannot retreat behind any system of laws, whether of nature or of history; he himself must be answerable. Herein lies the great opportunity of the future. Theories of every hue appeared to contradict it: world formulas and historical dialectics. Nevertheless, the future will depend on those who know and are ready to accept the all-decisive fact that man himself is responsible for the turn history will take and for whatever becomes of the world and of human existence. He can take the right turn or the wrong. To be able to choose the right, he must again desire that attitude which Plato long ago recognized as the epitome of human obligation, that which Scripture calls "the hunger and thirst" for justice. That is to say, he must recover the will to see the essence of things and to do "the right" that it demands.

In the preceding chapters we have frequently referred to the concept of dominion or government. If I am not mistaken, it is this concept which provides the practical point of reference towards which the lines of the emerging world-picture tend. Let us try to bring that picture into sharper focus.

What we see is a world which does not run itself, which must be led. Man's is no passive security in the world; he must dare to seize the initiative. What this world demands then, as a living correlative, is the genuine ruler.

The concept of ruler, like so many other vitally important ones, has been spoiled. To average contemporary ears the word "ruler" suggests a

meddlesome bureaucrat, an insulting totalitarian official, or some sort of specialist busied with things the
man in the street does not understand and hence mis-
trusts, something vaguely connected with the
socio-economic whole. Deep in the historical memory
stalks also the ghost of the ancient ruler of God-given
authority yet personal responsibility for justice and
welfare, an image which deteriorated into the most
questionable forms, ultimately into the modern concept of "the people" ruling in their own name.

Man's education today for the problems of public
office—the words given their full, original meaning
of *res publica*—must overcome these notions. What
we mean by "rule" is a human, ethical-spiritual attitude that is, above all, deeply conscious of how the
nascent world is conditioned and how every single
person, each in his or her place, may help to shape
it. Out of this consciousness comes awareness of the
monstrousness of the power at man's disposal and
the conviction that such power can be curbed by
responsibility alone. No constitutional clause, no
Supreme Court or local authority, no treaty will avail
unless the ordinary man feels that the fate of the *res
republica*, the common cause of human existence in
freedom and dignity, lies in his hands. He must realize further that it is criminal to allow the
apportionment of the great tasks facing the world to
be influenced by ambition, personal advantage, or
party politics. The only valid criterion should be:
What is to be done and who is best fitted to do it?
Rule, then, requires prudence; the ability to see the

manifoldness and interdependence of the factors at work; to "locate" again and again the so gravely imperilled golden mean on which not only the welfare, but the very subsistence of everything depends.[7]

[IV]

The structure of the world in the making, which we have attempted to sketch in a few very broad lines, is not founded on objective necessity, a "product" of a kind of cosmic-historical process; it is man-created. Such creativity, however, does not spring merely from rational considerations and utilitarian aims. The same "mind" that is in the objective goal must activate also those who effect it. Rather, the genuine *Weltbild* must be simultaneously effective within and without. It must be an integrated image of both man and his work. Hence the ultimate question must run: What are the features of the man who will determine the coming epoch? What his attitude, motives? Is there anything we can say about these?

Aside from a few constitutional optimists and those reassured by a fixed ideology, the people we meet everywhere today are marked by a profound anxiety. This is directed primarily at concrete political-historical possibilities, but reaches beyond them to the fundamental question: Is man still a match for his own works? During the course of the last century, man has

developed a measure of power far exceeding any previous dreams. This power has largely objectified itself
in scientific insights and forms of work that give rise to
constant new problems; in political structures that
look toward the future; in technical patterns which
seem to press ahead, propelled by their own
dynamism; finally, and above all, in the spiritual-intellectual attitudes of man himself, attitudes with a logic
of their own. The anxiety we mentioned questions
whether man is capable of handling all this in such a
way that he can endure with honor in fruitfulness and
joy; and it tends to answer, no. Man as he is today no
longer can meet such demands. His works and their
effects have outstripped him, making themselves independent. They have acquired *meta*-human, cosmic,
not to say demonic, characteristics which man can no
longer assimilate or direct.

That this feeling is based to some extent on fact
cannot be denied. We all know people who really are
no longer capable of controlling the modes of work
and life among which they have to live; who move
among them with a sense of alienation, submission,
capitulation. There are people—not a small number
either—who still feel at home in the era before the
great Time Divide which runs between the two World
Wars. Some of them manage to hold onto a little cor-
ner of existence in which they are still at ease; others
are at least able to create for themselves an interior
world of memories, books, and art. In the main, however, they are the defeated ones. But is that all? Or
does such defeat indicate more than the fate of one

particular generation caught fast in yesterday? Might not the trend toward objectivism in the development of human power mean that man has ceased to be the subject of history, that he has become a mere channel for processes beyond his reach? That he no longer controls power; rather, that power controls him?

If we equate mankind and contemporary man, the answer is, to say the least, dubious. But exactly at this point a hope emerges which cannot be easily defined. For one thing, its form is purely religious: it expresses itself in the confidence that God is greater than all historic processes; that these are in His hands, hence in His grace, and can at any time influence a world that was created, not to function like a machine, but likewise to create, in the living spirit.

Another hope is beginning to form deep in the womb of history. As we have seen, the mechanistic interpretation of existence is breaking down. Certainly, all happening is determined by cause; but there exists not only mechanistic causality, but also creative causality—not only causality unreeling necessity, but also spontaneous causality.[8] Effective even on the biological and physical levels, this kind of causality is decisive on the historical. Nothing is less realistic than the concept of a "necessary" historical process. Behind it stands not knowledge but a will apparent to anyone capable of learning from events, for that will has revealed itself in a manner that can only be described as metaphysical infamy. In reality, no one can estimate in advance the course history will take.

One can only step forward to meet it, shape it. History starts anew every minute as long as it is constantly determined anew in the freedom of every individual—but also as long as from its creative depths ever new structures and forms of events are born.

In the heyday of the modern age's personality-ideal, hopes would doubtless have been pinned on the great man, the genius with a mastery of power so perfect as to be a model for all men. We have only to put this idea into words to realize how utterly romantic it would sound today. Present conditions require not the single great genius, but a whole new human structure. This is no fantastic dream, but a reality that has recurred time and again in history. The chaos of the great migrations, which lasted half a millennium, was tamed by a type of man who could as well be termed the creator as product of the Middle Ages. When his era was over and his task accomplished, he was replaced by a new type—by the man who shouldered modernity and unleashed the monstrous masses of power which threaten us today. (He only unleashed them; he never mastered them. This is clear from the way he tried to justify the monstrousness of his seizures of nature and humanity with "utility" and "welfare.") Today the hope of the world is that a new type of man is coming into existence; one who does not succumb to the forces that have been liberated, but who is capable of bringing them to heel. This new man will have power not only over nature, but also over his own powers. In other words, he will understand how to subordinate power to the true meaning of human life and works. He will be the genuine "regent" who alone can save our age from going down in violence and chaos.

It is difficult to be more precise about this new world image without growing fanciful. All we can do is to collect the fragments of hints, hopes, experiments, miscarried developments, and try to make some sort of pattern.

The image thus pieced together is utopian, but there are two kinds of utopias: one of the playful ideal of fancy, the other a foreshadowing of things that should come. This latter kind has had real significance in history. It is impossible to explore in pure unknowing, nonhaving; we can seek only that which in some manner or other we already possess, be it only in dream or vision. Such "utopias" are attempts to provide a spiritual map for the world that is coming into being, that it may be sought effectively.

What, then, ought he to look like, the new human architect of that emergent world?

He must know and agree that the import of the coming culture is not welfare but dominion, fulfillment of man's God-given assignment to rule over the earth. What is needed is not universal insurance, but the kind of world in which human sovereignty with its greatness can express itself. This is not what the average citizen desired. He feared it, indeed, felt it to be a fundamentally wrong ideal. That is why he exercised the power he did possess with an uneasy conscience, feeling it necessary to justify it with "security," "utility," "welfare." That is why his governing is without a true ethos, why it has created no genuine government architecture, style, or tradition—because it has taken refuge in anonymity. The man we envision must unhesitatingly place security, utility, and welfare second; the greatness of the coming world image first.

With this we come to the second basic need: for an elemental relationship to technology. The creators of technology failed to assimilate their own creation into their sense of life. When a nineteenth-century industrialist built himself a house, the result was either a palace or a castle. The generation born between the World Wars feels differently. Here is a type of human being who lives in harmony with technology. With an ease that astounds nontechnical minds, he moves among the technical patterns of his day. Thus he possesses the freedom that is necessary if man is to prevail.

The new man we have in mind is also profoundly aware of the dangers inherent in present-day conditions. Since Hiroshima we know that we live on the rim of disaster, and that we shall stay there till the end of history. The new type of man senses the danger; he fears it too, naturally; but he does not succumb to that fear, for it is familiar to him. He has grown up with it.[9] He recognizes and faces it. In fact, it forms the kernel of a certain exhilarating sense of greatness. Current (in its extreme form "beatnik") contempt for bourgeois dependence on carefully precalculated security; the revolutionary change in man's relation to home and property; certain tendencies in modern art, philosophy and so forth—all seem to point that way. The man in question can live with danger, or at least knows that he can and must learn to. Yet he does not treat danger as a mere adventure; his typical reaction to it is a sense of responsibility for the world.

He has overcome the modern dogma: all things of themselves are for the best. For him the optimism of the progress-worshipper no longer exists. He knows from experience that left to themselves, things just as readily retrogress. He knows that the world is in the hands of freedom, hence he feels responsibility for tomorrow's kind of freedom. And love, his love of the world is very special, deepened by the precariousness, vulnerability, helplessness of his beloved. To his respect for power and greatness, his comfortable relationships to technology and his will to utilize it, to the zest of looking danger in the eye, he adds another quality, chivalry, not to say tenderness, toward finite, oh-so-jeopardized existence.

A further trait is his acceptance of absolute demands. The coming man is definitely un-liberal, which does not mean that he has no respect for freedom. The "liberal" attitude is that which declines to incorporate absolutes into existence because their either-or engenders struggle. It is far easier to be able to see things in any light, "the only important thing" being "life" and "getting along with others." Values and ideas are but a matter of personal opinion. Leave everybody alone, and all will be well. The man under discussion knows that unfreed from such attitudes man can never cope with the existential situation we face today. What will count will be not details or elaborations, but fundamentals: dignity or slavery; growth or decline; truth or lie; the mind or the passions.

This man knows how to command as well as how to obey. He respects discipline not as a passive, blind "being integrated into" a system, but the responsible discipline which stems from his own conscience and personal honor. Here is the prerequisite for the greatest task he faces: that of establishing an authority which respects human dignity, of creating a social order in which the person can exist. The ability to command and to obey has been lost in the degree that faith and doctrine have disappeared from man's consciousness. As a result, in the place of unconditional truth, we have catchwords: instead of command, compulsion; instead of obedience, self-abandonment. What real command and real obedience are must be rediscovered. This is possible only when absolute sovereignty is recognized, absolute values are accepted; in other words, when God is acknowledged as the living norm and point of reference for all existence. Ultimately, one can command only from God, obey only in Him.

The new man also appreciates asceticism again. He knows that there is no authority which does not begin with the command of self, that no orderly form of existence can be established by anyone who is not, himself, "formed." There is no greatness which is not grounded deep in self-conquest and self-denial.

t of themselves orderly; they t) in order. Man must master aith in the so-called goodness . It is a refusal to face the evil with the good. Thus the good rnestness. The evil in nature this resistance is asceticism. mand, which stems not from thority; real, unqualified obe— not self-abandonment but nate competence—these are n overcomes the direct impact clinations. The man to come r that liberating power lies in rdly accepted suffering trans— d that all existential growth depends not on effort alone, but also on freely offered sacrifice.

Relevant to this is something we have glimpsed at various points—namely, companionship between man and man. Not the respectless familiarity of barracks and camp. Also not the tired remnants of that ethos which insists that life's challenges are meaningless and that all grounds of confidence, greatness, and joy have crumbled away. But the natural solidarity of those who stand shoulder to shoulder at the common task, in common danger. It is the self-understood readiness for mutual help and for the integration of individual efforts. It also possesses that unqualified character often engendered by and transcending the particular bonds of blood and sympathy.[10]

From what has been said it must be clear that what is needed is not a new version of Sparta. The new type of man is as apt to be a soldier as he is to be a priest, a businessman as a farmer, a doctor as an artist, a factory worker as a research scientist. He certainly must not be appraised by his toughness alone. All too many in Germany fell victim not so long ago to the "heroic" ideals of "fanatic will," "dogged determination," "ruthless sacrifice"! Those who tossed these slogans about so freely were in reality not strong but weak: they were violent from personal uncertainty, brutal from paucity of heart. And if they actually were fearless in the face of danger, it was because for them the spirit counted as nothing. The strength we mean comes straight from the spirit, from the heart's voluntary surrender; that is why it nurtures all that is known as reverence, magnanimity, goodness, considerateness, interiority.

One final trait in this image of man: his religious attitude.

Should the possibility of a world dominion such as we have tried to suggest be felt, generally, an objective, this-worldly will to work and to govern might come into existence which would reject everything metaphysical as obstructive. But, even then, the tremendousness of the task ahead would force people to take reality seriously, and this in turn would lead to the realization that the world can be mastered only along the lines of truth, whole truth, hence in obedience to the essence of things.

Precisely here, in such obedience, lies the seed of a very real piety. The mind which considers reality not from any subjective *a priori*, but purely objectively, is more inclined than the subjective, unscientific, undisciplined mind to discover that finiteness is also createdness. It has been prepared to grasp the revealed nature of everything that is, and from there to reach a decisive affirmation of Biblical Revelation.[11] By this process a completely unsentimental, in the purest sense of the word, realistic piety would evolve, a piety no longer operating in a separate realm of psychological interiority or religious idealism, but within reality, a reality which, because complete, is also the reality created, sustained, and willed by God.

From the depths of clarity such as this the new man would also be able to see through the illusions which reign in the midst of scientific and technological development: the deception behind the "liberal's" idolatry of culture, behind the totalitarian's utopia, the tragicist's pessimism; behind modern mythicism and the hermaphrodite world of psychoanalysis. He would see and know for himself: Reality simply is not like that! These paths lead away from, not to it. Man is not so constructed, and neither is life. We may place high hope in the power of direct insight which belongs to this new realism.

Moreover, the objective mind seems to run a good chance of grasping Christianity's inmost secret: humility. To appreciate its transforming power—truly an intellectual-spiritual splitting of the existential atom— to make it the extricating energy for life's seemingly inextricable tangle.

From all this could come something like true dominion.

More or less along these lines we might trace the portrait of the human type on whom the hopes and presentiments of our age converge. It is a very sketchy sketch; after all, we are attempting to portray features still only hoped for. It is an utopia, yes, but possibly the right kind.

We must not forget that the portrait is of a man by a man. To attempt that of a woman is a woman's task—unless a man were to take it upon himself to tell woman how he would wish her to be: not only how his senses would be pleased to fancy her, but above all, his mind and his heart, the center of his human essence. Similarly, a woman might well give us her conception of the real man. This would not be a bad approach to the dialog. Perhaps at some points it has already begun: in the discussion on social work, literature, drama, art, education. Unfortunately, it is sometimes difficult to distinguish between genuine exchange and mere discussion grounded on misunderstanding, resentment, vanity, intellectual fashions, and bluff.

NOTES

1. See section one, *The End of the Modern World.*

2. "A few hours before the opening of the San Francisco Conference on the peace with Japan, President Truman announced that the United States possessed new weapons more powerful than the atomic bomb. In a general war these could wipe out civilization altogether." Naturally, the tactical pur-

pose of such statements should not be ignored. Nevertheless, coming from the statesman ultimately responsible for the initiative of the entire West, it gives us pause.

3. See Guardini, "Auf der Suche nach dem Frieden," *Hochland,* 41st year, Vol. II.

4. We do well to listen to the speech around us. Its general condition, the words it employs or self-consciously avoids, reveal much about the age it is expressing. The use of words like these in reference to human beings is all too revealing.

5. The various characteristics of the coming world order as described up to this point merge one into the other, but I have deliberately drawn the picture in that way, in order to show various aspects of one and the same thing—the particular aggregate form, so to speak, of the coming existence, and the way I believe it will be seen to develop and become effective.

6. Space does not allow us to discuss the difficulties involved in defining these poles or the dangers of a new monism.

7. Only in this sense, and not in any dogma of equality, lies the true meaning of "democracy."

8. In this connection, see Guardini, *Freiheit, Gnade, Schicksal* (1948), pp. 113ff.

9. It would be valuable to ascertain whether the sense of fear which permeates our age is shared by all or, for example, only by those who feel basically at home in the period before the Time Divide and not in today. This does not imply that those who do "belong" to their own era do not feel themselves threatened by its political, economic, sociological dangers. But is such realistic fear the same as that crippling, form-and-substance-consuming panic which overcomes those no longer at ease in the world?

10. The demands of neighborliness also build a spirit of helpfulness transcending personal sympathies and antipathies.

11. Compare Guardini, *Die Sinne und die religiöse Erkenntnis* (Würzburg, 1950).

CHAPTER EIGHT

POSSIBILITIES OF ACTION

[I]

In view of the circumstances we have described, threatened man asks what he, today, could do.

Obviously, political decisions on foreign and domestic policy are important; important too are the solution of economic and social problems, the improvement of the school system, the tremendous tasks confronting scientific research and the arts, the assimilation of refugees, and so forth.

It is of course out of the question to deal with them all within the limits of this study. We should do better to concentrate on that from which, ultimately, all action or refraining from action receives its direction: personal perception, judgment, and decision, as well as the problems of education connected with these.

Modern man, whom we have discussed at some length, likes to consider history as the unreeling of a necessary process. This view is an after-effect of the modern conception of nature as the basic data of that which is. If this is true, then it must follow that all that takes place in nature is natural, hence right. Now actually, history is determined by the spirit, but according to the above theory, even the spirit is a mere part of that universal whole whose "rightness" finds expression within the framework of nature. Therefore, all the mistakes, abuses, violence of individuals in history are scrupulously ignored: the process of history is a "natural" process, hence right and trustworthy.

One of the main decisions which future man will have to make will turn on his realizing or failing to realize the error of this concept. Man is determined by the spirit; but the spirit is *not* "nature." The spirit lives and acts neither by historical nor by metaphysical necessity, but of its own impulse. It is free. It draws its ultimate life and health from its right relation to the true and the good, a relation which it is also free to deny or destroy. Man does not belong exclusively to the world; rather he stands on its borders, at once in the world yet outside it, integrated into it yet simultaneously dealing with it because he is related directly to God. Not to the "Spirit of the Age," not to the "All-Mysterious One," not to any First Cause—but to the sovereign Lord, Creator of all being, who called man into existence and sustains him in that vocation, who gave the world into his keeping, and who will demand an account of what he has done with it.

Thus history does not run on its own; it is run. It can also be run badly. And not only in view of certain decisions or for certain stretches of the road and in certain areas; its whole direction can be off course for whole epochs, centuries long. This we know or at least suspect, for all our confidence in our experimental and theoretical precision. It is this "suspicion" which gives our situation its special poignancy.

Man is being given ever more power of decision and control over world reality, but man himself is removing himself farther and farther from the norms which spring from the truth of being and from the demands of goodness and holiness. Thus his decisions are in danger of becoming increasingly fortuitous.

For this reason the basic answer to the question "What can be done?" must run something like this. First of all, man must accept the full measure of his responsibility; but to be able to do this, he must regain his right relation to the truth of things, to the demands of his own deepest self, and finally to God. Otherwise he becomes the victim of his own power, and the forecast of "global catastrophe" quoted earlier will really become inevitable.

When we said that the spirit is not determined by natural necessity but must act in freedom, we did not mean that man himself must establish the meaning of events. It is worth noting that both extreme existentialism and the totalitarian state believe that he must, thus proclaiming themselves opposite poles of the same basic will: to use power arbitrarily, which means to misuse it as violence. In reality, everything that exists is shaped in a meaningful form which provides acting man with the norm from which to draw the possible and the right. Freedom does not consist in following our personal or political predilections, but in doing what is required by the essence of things.

All this means first of all that we must know where the historical changes discussed above are leading; we must ascertain their underlying causes and face the problems they involve. This is the task to which school and university must apply themselves if they are not to fall by the wayside of time. Important too are those forms of research and effort which have developed along with the pedagogical labors of the last fifty years and which have consolidated in vocational workshops, holiday conferences, academies, and various special institutes. The sociological "place" of such attempts at better understanding lies between school and university, between the individual quest and consolidated research efforts of the profession. Thus they are well suited for the task of tracing forces in the making, and responsible authorities have good reason to encourage them. Not to influence them, for that would only destroy the opportunities peculiar to free experiment; but to allow for them, to support them and to cooperate with them in a form which remains to be found.

The modern age was inclined to grapple with necessary innovations by means of rational intellect and organization. The problems which face us today are so gigantic that we must reach for a deeper hold.

Now that science has begun to break up the natural elements, something analogous must take place on the human level: man must examine the basic facts of his existence. If he does not, events will pass him by, leaving him an ever greater stranger on earth. In the main, men agree that technology, economics, politics must be directed "realistically," but what they mean is in a manner which totally disregards ultimate values: man's personal destiny and all that is God's due. This lopsided attitude is just as unrealistic and out-of-date as that which regards the phenomenon of illness only physically, ignoring its psychological-biological aspects. Medicine is coming to realize ever more clearly to what extent the soul determines the body's health or illness, and that only the diagnosis which encompasses the patient's whole reality, including his spiritual-intellectual life, can really claim to be realistic. The same is true here. Already not a few people listen with neither derision nor skepticism when the pains of our age are diagnosed clearly: what the sick world needs is a *metanoia*, a conversion, a reappraisal of our whole attitude toward life, accompanied by a fundamental change in the "climate" in which people and things are appraised. It is to them, those in search of a genuine realism, that the following is addressed.

Let us be explicit. Have we ever stopped to consider exactly what takes place when the average superior assigns a task to a subordinate...when the average school teacher teaches a class or maintains discipline...judge decides a case...priest champions the things of God...doctor treats a patient...bureaucrat deals with the public in his office...industrialist directs his firm...merchant supplies his customers...factory-worker tends his machine...farmer runs his farm? Is it really clear to us in each concrete process what the decisive intention and attitude was, and what its direct and indirect results? Was the truth in each case protected? Its particular validity trusted? Did the person encountered go away feeling that he had been treated with dignity, that he had been received as a person by a person? Did that other appeal to his freedom, to all that is vital and creative to him? Together did they reach the heart of the matter, broaching it as it was meant to be broached, essentially?

The objection that these are private matters of no historical importance does not hold. Every historical process, even the most dynamic, is made up of just such situations, and the way they are dealt with is what gives each phase of history its particular mold. It is exactly here that the shoe we are wearing pinches: these elementary things, which we ought to be able to take for granted, we no longer can take for granted. Of course, in earlier epochs also truth, justice, personal dignity, and contact with others' central creativity were not always, possibly not even generally, protected; but they certainly were acknowledged and at least in theory taken seriously. The tendency to respect them was there, and the man of good will could easily, at any time, step from the general acknowledgment of their importance to his own particular realization of them. This has changed—to our culture's growing uneasiness. The lack of human warmth and dignity in our contacts with "the world" is what chills the heart, and what lurks at the bottom of the growing feeling that things are no longer "right." The fact must be recognized and accepted that even the most commonplace "public relations" are *not* a matter of private morality, but the life blood of every historical process and public policy, and that on them will depend the health or death of our political and cultural existence.

[II]

Let us attempt the difficult and thankless task of suggesting a few practical points of view.

Essential to any really practical suggestion is its workability, so let us try to get down to brass tacks, even at the risk of sounding "moralistic." Actually, many people, the most dispassionate and unbiased realists included, continue to live according to much-abused "morality," and it is they, not the "free spirits," who uphold existence.

First, we must try to rediscover something of what is called the contemplative attitude, actually experience it ourselves, not just talk about it interestingly. All around us we see activity, organization, operations of every possible type; but what directs them? An inwardness no longer really at home within itself; which thinks, judges, acts from the surface, guided by mere intellect, utility, and the impulses of power, property, and pleasure. An "interiority" too superficial to contact the truth lying at life's center; which no longer reaches the essential and everlasting, but remains somewhere just under the skin-level of the provisional and the fortuitous.

Before all else, then, man's depths must be reawakened. His life must again include times, his day moments of stillness in which he collects himself, spreads out before his heart the problems which have stirred him during the day. In a word, man must learn again to meditate and to pray. How, we cannot say. This depends largely on his basic beliefs, his religious position, his temperament and surroundings. But in any case, he must step aside from the general hustle and bustle; must become tranquil and really "there," opening his mind and heart wide to some word of piety or wisdom or ethical honor, whether he takes it from Scripture or Plato, from Goethe or Jeremias Gotthelf. He must accept the criticism which that particular word suggests to him, examining some related aspect of his own life in its beam. Only an attitude this deeply grounded in truth can gain a stand against the forces around us.[1]

Next, we must pose the elementary question as to the essence of things.

One look is enough to reveal how schematic is our attitude to things; what slaves of convention we are; how superficially—from the criteria of mere advantage, ease, and time-saving—we approach things. Yet each thing has an essence. When this is ignored or abused, a resistance is built up which neither cunning nor violence can overcome. Then reality bolts its doors against man's grasp. The order of things is destroyed. The axles of the economic, social, political wagons run hot. No, man cannot use things as he pleases, at least not generally and not for long. He can use them only essentially, as they were meant to be used, with impunity. Otherwise he invites catastro-

phe. Anyone who uses his eyes can see the catastrophic results of mishandled reality.

Therefore we must return to the essence of being
and ask: What is the connection between a man's
work and his life? What must justice and law be like if
they are to further rather than hinder? What is property, its rights, its abuses? What is genuine command
and what makes it possible? What is obedience, and
how is it related to freedom? What do health, sickness, death really signify? What friendship,
comradeship? When may attraction claim the high
name of love? What does the union of man and
woman known as marriage mean? (At present something so seedy, so choked with weed, that few people
seem to have any serious conception of it, although it
is the bearer of all human existence.) Does such a
thing as a scale of values exist? Which of its values is
the most important, which the least?

These are the elemental realities we live from, for,
with. We deal with them constantly, arrange and
reshape them—but do we know what they are?
Apparently not, or we would not treat them so casu-
ally. So we had better find out what they are, and not
merely with a detached rationality, but by penetrating
them so deeply that we are shaken by their power and
significance.[2]

Further, we must learn again that command over
the world presupposes command of self. For how can
men control the growing monstrousness of power
when they cannot even control their own appetites?

How can they shape political or cultural decisions affecting countless others, when they are continually failing themselves?

There was a time when philosophers, historians, and poets used the word "asceticism" as an expression of "medieval hostility to life," and advocated instead a life lived in search of "experience," of immediate sensation. Today much of this has changed, at least with those whose thinking and judging stem from responsibility. At any rate, we do well to realize at last that there has never been greatness without asceticism, and what is needed today is something not only great, but ultimate: we must decide whether we are going to realize the requirements of rule in freedom or in slavery.

An ascetic is a man who has himself well in hand. To be capable of this, he must recognize the wrongs within himself and set about righting them. He must regulate his physical as well as his intellectual appetites, educate himself to hold his possessions in freedom, sacrificing the lesser for the greater. He must fight for inner health and freedom—against the machinations of advertising, the flood of loud sensationalism, against noise in all its forms. He must acquire a certain distance from things; must train himself to think independently, to resist what "they" say. Street, traffic, newspaper, radio, screen, and television all present problems of self-discipline, indeed of the most elementary self-defense—problems we hardly suspect, to say nothing of tackling. Everywhere man is capitulating to the forces of barbarism. Asceticism is the refusal to capitulate, the determination to fight them, there at the key bastion—namely, in ourselves.[3] It means that through self-discipline and self-restraint he develops from the core outward, holding life high in honor so that it may be fruitful on the level of its deepest significance.

Further, we must weigh again, in all earnestness, the existential question of our ultimate relation to God.

Man is not so constructed as to be complete in himself and, in addition, capable of entering into relations with God or not as he sees fit; his very essence consists in his relation to God. The only kind of man that exists is man-in-relation-to-God; and what he understands by that relationship, how seriously he takes it, and what he does about it are the determining factors of his character. This is so, and no philosopher, politician, poet, or psychologist can change it.

It is dangerous to ignore realities, for they have a way of avenging themselves. When instincts are suppressed or conflicts kept alive, neuroses set in. God is the Reality on whom all other realities, including the human, are founded. When existence fails to give Him His due, existence sickens.

Finally: Do everything that is to be done with respect for the truth, and do it in freedom of spirit, in spite of the obstacles within and without, and in the teeth of selfishness, sloth, cowardice, popular opinion. And do it with confidence!

By this I do not mean to follow a program of any

kind, but to make the simple responses that always were and always will be right: Not to wait until someone in need asks for help, but to offer it; to perform every official act in a manner befitting both common sense and human dignity; to declare a truth when its "hour" has come, even when it will bring down opposition or ridicule; to accept responsibility when the conscience considers it a duty.

When one so acts, he paves a road, which, followed with sincerity and courage, leads far, no one can say how far, into the realm where the great things of Time are decided.

It may seem strange that our consideration of universal problems should end on the most personal level possible. But as the subtitle of *Power and Responsibility* indicates, it is an attempt to set a course. What would be the sense of developing ideas while ignoring the point from which they can be realized or fail to be realized? It cannot have escaped the reader that in these pages we have not tried to present programs or panaceas, but to free the initiative for fruitful action.

NOTES

1. Perhaps, in this connection, I may be permitted to call attention to my *Prayer in Practice* (New York: Pantheon, 1957).

2. Most illuminating on this subject are the writings of Josef Pieper, whose *Musse und Kult* (1948)—translated as *Leisure, the Basis of Culture* (New York: Pantheon, 1952)—and *Über das Schweigen Goethes* (1951) are little masterpieces. Also see Otto Bollnow, *Einfache Sittlichkeit* (Göttingen, 1947). And not to be forgotten are two books that appeared long ago and have not been surpassed: Fr. W. Foerster's *Lebenskunde* (1904 ff.) and *Lebensführung*

(1909 ff.)

3. One small but staggering example. A well-known Hamburg newspaper, *Die Zeit*, reported that a modern radio-dramatist, secretly, by night, lowered a microphone in front of the open bedroom window of an elderly couple who lived in the´apartment below him. The North Western German Radio then broadcast the matrimonial quarrel-scene along with other micro-phonic "candid shots" from everyday life. Apparently, not without certain misgivings. However, these were not moral but only juridical; they vanished when the dramatist produced convincing evidence that all the people on whom he had eavesdropped, and whose intimacies he had violated with his tapes, had given him permission to broadcast them—in writing. Here is one such capitulation. What the incentives behind it were is another ques-tion. Whatever it was, to borrow the editor's adjectives, they were "astonishing and terrifying," the more so as the public accepted the "joke" without a murmur. Here is but one indication among countless of how far the spineless man of our day has already sunk. Isn't it proof enough that human totalitarianism, the total surrender of man's last vestiges of privacy and dignity, is already with us? Now do we see where asceticism comes in? In the struggle against mankind's traitor within man himself? And do we realize at last that he is not to be downed with gentle idealism and faith in "the goodness of human nature"?